Canada's
Covered Bridges
by
Harold Stiver

Copyright Statement

Canada's Covered Bridges
A Guide for Photographers and Explorers

ISBN #978-1-927835-42-5

Table of Contents

New Brunswick Bridge Tours

Ontario Covered Bridges

Quebec Covered Bridges

How to use this Book

For each of the 150 historical or Traditional Covered Bridges remaining in Canada, we have included photographs as well as descriptive and statistical data. Traditional Covered Bridges are those that follow the building practices of the Nineteenth Century and the early part of the Twentieth Century or those built later that follow those methods. All of these bridges have had repairs done as portions wear out, and some may have been almost entirely replaced through the years. I have used "The National Society for the Preservation of Covered Bridges, Inc." list of what they consider as Traditional Bridges.

Following is data included for each bridge

Name: This is listed in bold type, and where there are other names, it is the common name or the name listed on an accompanying plaque.

Other Names: Underneath the Common Name in brackets, you will find other names that the bridge has been known by.

Nearest Region and Township are listed.

It is frustrating to go on an excursion to see something and not be able to find it. This book offers you multiple ways to ensure that doesn't happen.

GPS Position: This is our recommended method. Enter the coordinates in a good GPS unit and it should take you right there. You, of course, must use care that you are not led off road or on a dangerous route.

Detailed Driving Directions: Directions from a town near to the bridge.

Builder: If known, the name of the original builder(s) is listed.

Year Built: As well as the year built, if it has been moved it will shown with the year preceded by the letter M and, if a major repair has been done, the year will be shown preceded by the letter R.

Truss Type: The type for the particular bridge will be listed. If you are interested in more information on the various types of trusses, access "Truss Types" from the Table of Contents.

Dimensions: The length and number of spans

Notes: A place where you can find additional items of interest about the bridge.

World Index Number:
Covered bridges are assigned a number to keep track of them which consists of three numbers separated by hyphens.

The first number represents the number of the U.S. State in alphabetical order. Following number 50 for the 50th state are additional numbers for Canadian provinces. Thus the numbers 05 represents California.

The second set of numbers represents the Region of that state, again based on alphabetical order. Humboldt is the 12th Region alphabetically in California, and it is designated as 05-12.

Each bridge in that Region is given a number as it was discovered or built. Zane's Ranch was the fifth bridge discovered or built in the Region of Humboldt, California and it therefore has the designation of 05-12-05. Sometimes you will see the first set of numbers replaced by the abbreviation for the state, thus CA-12-05.

A bridge is sometimes substantially rebuilt or replaced and it then has the suffix #2 added to it.

Photographing Covered Bridges

Some standard positions
Portal: Taken to show the ends of bridge or bridge opening. This view, usually symmetrical, will include various signs posted. This is also a good way to get run over, so be careful!
3/4 view: Shows both the front and sides of the bridge, and is often the most attractive.
Side view: Taken from a bank or from the river, this gives not only a nice view of the bridge but usually allows for some interesting foreground elements.
Interior view: An image taken from the interior of the bridge will show some interesting structure but there is not a lot of available light. A tripod is important and HDR processing is helpful.
Landscape View: With the bridge smaller in the frame, you can introduce the habitat around it, particularly effective with colorful autumn foliage.

Using HDR(High Dynamic Range)
HDR is a process where multiple images of varying exposure are combined to make one image.

It has a bad name with some people because many HDR images are super-saturated, a kind of digital age version of an Elvis painted on velvet. However, the process is actually about getting a full range of exposure with no burnt out highlights or blocked shadows. This is an ideal processing solution for photographing Covered Bridges where you often have open light sky set against dark shadowed landscape and structure.

I use a series of three exposures at levels of -1 2/3, 0, +1 2/3, and this normally runs the full exposure range encountered. It is important to use a stable tripod.

One situation where you may need a larger series is shooting from within a bridge and using the window to frame an outside scene. The dynamic range is huge and you will need to have a series with a much larger range.

There are a number of software programs you can use to combine these images including newer editions of Photoshop. I use Photomatix which I have found very versatile and easy to use.

Best times for photographing bridges

Mornings and evenings are generally the best times for outdoor photography but the use of HDR processing makes it easier even in bright direct light. Although any season is good for bridge photography including the winter, fall foliage included in a scene can be spectacular.

A Short History of Covered Bridges

Let's deal with that often posed question; "Why were the bridges covered"

1. Crossing animals thought it was a barn and entered easily. I like this suggestion, it shows imagination. However, its not the answer although the original bridges normally had no windows and this is said to be because animals would not be spooked by the sight of the water.

2. To cover up the unsightly truss structure. I don't think those early pioneers were that sensitive, and personally, I like the look of the trusses.

3. To keep snow off the travelled portion. In fact the bridge owners often paid to have the insides "snowed" in order to facilitate sleighs.

4. It offered some privacy to courting couples, hence "kissing bridges". That is a nice romantic notion but no.

In fact, the bridge was covered for economic reasons. The truss system was where much of the bridge's cost was found, and if left open to the elements, it deteriorated and the bridge became unstable and unsafe. Covering it protected this valuable portion and the roof could be replaced as needed with inexpensive materials and unskilled labour. Without coverings, a bridge might only have a life span of a decade while one that was covered often lasted 75 years or more before repairs became necessary. Besides extending the longevity of a bridge, wooden covered bridges had the virtue that they could be constructed of local materials and there were many available workers skilled in working with wood.

The first known Covered Bridge in North America was built in 1804 by Theodore Burr. It was called the Waterford bridge and it spanned the Hudson River in New York.

For the rest of the century and into the 20th Century, Covered bridge building boomed as the country became populated and people needed to travel between communities. The cost of constructing and maintaining a bridge was normally borne by the nearby community and many bridges charged a toll as a method of offsetting these costs.

The period from 1825 to 1875 was the heyday of bridge building but near the end of that period iron bridges began to supplant them.

The number of Covered bridges may have numbered 10,000 but have now dropped to about 840 spread throughout North America. Many have Historical Designations which provides them protection and many communities are interested in protecting their local historical bridges.

British Columbia Regional Map

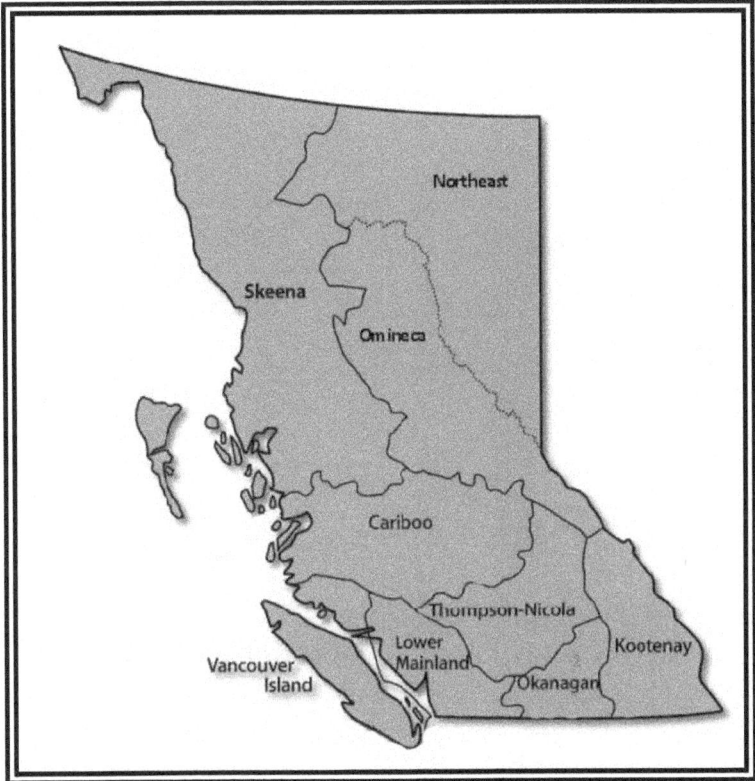

Kicking Horse Pedestrian Covered Bridge
Region: Columbia-Shuswap, British Columbia
Township: Golden

GPS Position: 51°17'58.9"N 116°58'06.2"W
Directions: From Golden, head north on 10th Ave S/BC-95 N for 700 m and turn left onto 6 St N. After 180 m turn left onto 8th Ave N and the bridge
Crosses: Kicking Horse River
Carries: 8th Ave N
Builder: Timber Framers Guild
Year Built: 2001
Truss Type: Multiple King (Double) and Arch
Dimensions: 1 Span, 46 meters, 150 feet

Notes: A local project of the Timber Framers Guild whose volunteers completed the project in 2001

World Index Number: BC/52-08-02
National Register of Historic Places: Not listed

Ashnola River Road (Red) Covered Bridge
Region: Okanagan-Similkameen, British Columbia
Township: Keremeos

GPS Position: 49°12'14.4"N 119°53'18.6"W
Directions: From Keremeos, head west on BC-3 W for 3.2 km and turn left onto Ashnola Rd where the bridge is 600 m
Crosses: Similkameen River
Carries: Ashnola Rd

Builder: Vancouver Victoria & Eastern Railway
Year Built: 1923
Truss Type: Howe
Dimensions: 3 Span, 122 meters, 400 feet

Notes: *This beautiful historic structure was destroyed in a fire shortly before this guide was published*

World Index Number: BC/52-21-02
National Register of Historic Places: Not listed

New Brunswick County Map

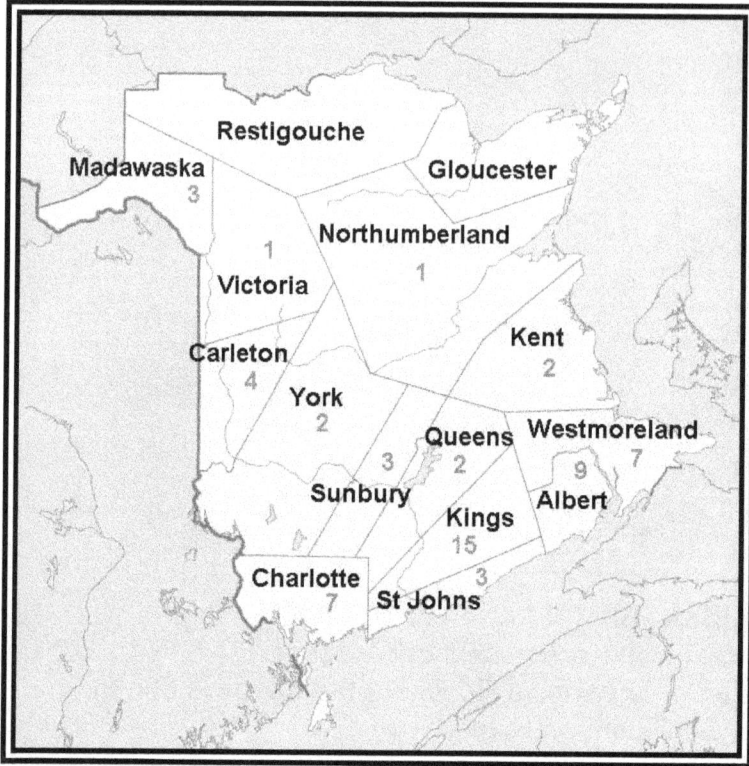

Restigouche

Madawaska
3

Gloucester

Northumberland
1

Victoria
1

Carleton
4

York
2

Kent
2

Queens
2

Westmoreland
7

Sunbury
3

Albert
9

Kings
15

Charlotte
7

St Johns
3

The World's Longest Covered Bridge

The Hartland Covered Bridge crosses the Saint John River from Hartland to Somerville, New Brunswick. At 391 meters (1282 feet), it is the longest covered bridge in the world.

However it wasn't always covered. Before the bridge was built, the river could only be crossed by ferry.

Planning and construction for the structure began in 1898 with the work to be performed by the newly formed Hartford Bridge Company. By 1901, the construction was completed and the official opening was made on July 4, 1901 with thousands of people attending.

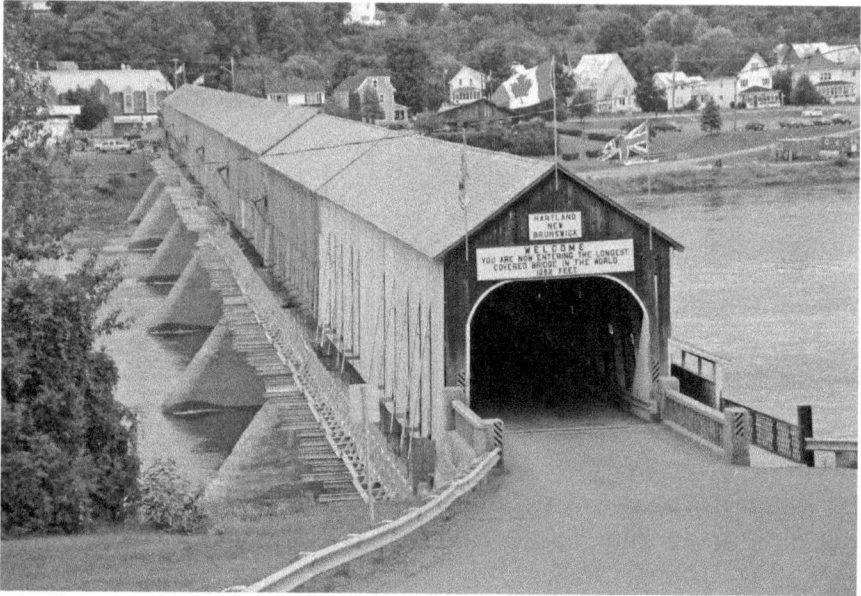

A local doctor had already crossed some weeks earlier to answer an emergency call. Workers are said to have placed planks on the deck to allow him to drive his car across.

The bridge was initially funded by tolls but this was discontinued in 1906 when it was purchased by the provincial government.

The bridge was covered in 1921-22, although not without some controversy as it was suggested that it would damage the young people's morals. This was a reference to the notion of a "kissing bridge" where couples would stop under cover of the bridge.

Covering the bridge involved seven spans with Howe trusses. The original piers were of stone filled cribwork and these were replaced by concrete ones. Lighting was installed in 1924 and a side walkway was added to the bridge in 1945.

The bridge has suffered a few calamities. A 1907 fire damaged the structure and in 1920 two spans collapsed from ice jams. In 1966 there was an attempt to burn it and in 1982 vehicle damage caused its closure for a few months.

The bridge was declared a National Historic Site in 1980, and a Provincial Historic Site in 1999

In 1987 the Olympic Torch for the 1988 Winter Olympics was carried across the bridge and a Canadian postage stamp was issued honouring the bridge in 1995.

Bamford-Colpitts Covered Bridge
County: Albert, New Brunswick
Township: Coverdale

GPS Position: 45°59'18.0"N 64°58'25.6"W
Directions: From Colpitts Settlement, head northwest on NB-895 N for 0.7 km and the bridge is on the right
Crosses: Kicking Horse River
Carries: Bypassed section
Builder: Not known
Year Built: 1941
Truss Type: Burr Variation
Dimensions: 1 span, 32 meters, 103 feet
Notes: It is in a quiet country setting. It is on private property but there are easy setups nearby to obtain pictures. There are advertisements painted on the interior which are interesting

World Index Number: NB/55-01-01
National Register of Historic Places: Not listed

Crooked Creek #3 Covered Bridge
County: Albert, New Brunswick
Township: Hopewell

GPS Position: 45°47'49.2"N 64°46'36.1"W
Directions: From Riverside-Albert, head north on Forestdale Rd for 0.8 km and continue onto Crooked Creek Rd where the bridge is 5.9 km
Crosses: Crooked Creek
Carries: Crooked Creek Road
Builder: Not known
Year Built: 1945
Truss Type: Howe and Queen
Dimensions: 1 span, 28 meters, 94 feet
Notes: Crooked Creek Road can be very rough, especially after a recent rain and you need to walk the last 0.5 km. The setting is exceptional in the fall
World Index Number: NB/55-01-03
National Register of Historic Places: Not listed

Lower Forty Five River #1 Covered Bridge
County: Albert, New Brunswick
Township: Alma

GPS Position: 45°41'13.2"N 64°57'10.8"W
Directions: From Teehans Corner, head south on 45 Rd and the bridge is found in 2.5 km
Crosses: Forty Five River
Carries: 45 Road
Builder: Alex Garland
Year Built: 1914
Truss Type: Howe and Queen
Dimensions: 1 span, 30 meters, 102 feet
Notes: Located on the eastern side of Fundy National Park. Like many New Brunswick bridges, it is unpainted and without windows

World Index Number: NB/55-01-04
National Register of Historic Places: Not listed

Point Wolfe Covered Bridge
County: Albert, New Brunswick
Township: Alma

GPS Position: 45°33'02.5"N 65°00'46.8"W
Directions: From Highway 114 south of Alma, head south on Point Wolfe Rd for 7.4 km to find the bridge
Crosses: Point Wolfe River
Carries: Point Wolfe Road
Builder: Not known
Year Built: 1992
Truss Type: Howe and Queen
Dimensions: 1 span, 29 meters, 95 feet
Notes: Unlike most of New Brunswick's Covered Bridges, Point Wolfe is painted and the red colour looks great in front of the green background

World Index Number: NB/55-01-05#2
National Register of Historic Places: Not listed

Peter Jonah Covered Bridge
County: Albert, New Brunswick
Township: Hillsboro

GPS Position: 46°00'10.4"N 64°54'00.7"W
Directions: From the town of Turtle Creek, head northwest on NB-910 N toward NB Trail for 4.6 km and continue straight onto Dewey Rd to find the bridge
Crosses: Pond
Carries: Dewey Road
Builder: Not known
Year Built: 1912 (M2013)
Truss Type: Multiple King and Queen
Dimensions: 1 span, 20.7 meters, 68 feet
Notes: The bridge was moved due to a new reservoir for the Moncton water supply was built. Have a look at the interesting hip or cottage roof
World Index Number: NB/55-01-07
National Register of Historic Places: Not listed

Germantown Lake CB (Shepody River #3)
County: Albert, New Brunswick
Township: Harvey

GPS Position: 45°40'00.1"N 64°48'40.7"W
Directions: From the town of Germantown, head southeast
on Midway Rd for 0.4 km to find the bridge
Crosses: Shepody River
Carries: Midway Road

Builder: Not known
Year Built: 1903
Truss Type: Howe and Queen
Dimensions: 1 span, 19 meters, 60 feet
Notes: The bridge is in a quiet rural setting at the south end of
Shepody National Wildlife Area

World Index Number: NB/55-01-08
National Register of Historic Places: Not listed

Hartley Steeves CB (Weldon Creek #3)
County: Albert, New Brunswick
Township: Hillsboro

GPS Position: 45°55'01.9"N 64°42'03.6"W
Directions: From Isaiah Corner, head northeast on NB-910 S for 1.9 km and find the bridge
Crosses: Weldon Creek
Carries: NB-910
Builder: John Forbes
Year Built: 1923
Truss Type: Howe and Queen
Dimensions: 1 span, 19 meters, 63 feet
Notes: This bridge used to have a companion nearby, the Harris Steeves Covered Bridge which was destroyed 30 years ago. It is in a great setting, especially in the fall,

World Index Number: NB/55-01-11
National Register of Historic Places: Not listed

Sawmill Creek Mouth CB (Sawmill Creek #1)
County: Albert, New Brunswick
Township: Hopewell

GPS Position: 45°45'52.9"N 64°41'33.0"W
Directions: From Hopewell Hill, head west on Main St/NB-114 S for 0.8 km to the bridge
Crosses: Sawmill Creek
Carries: Main St/NB-114 S (Bypassed)

Builder: Albert E. Smye
Year Built: 1907 (R2021)
Truss Type: Howe and Queen
Dimensions: 1 span, 32 meters, 105 feet
Notes: The structure had major deficiencies but the 2021 repairs have it in good shape. It was bypassed in the 1960s.

World Index Number: NB/55-01-20
National Register of Historic Places: Not listed

William Mitton Covered Bridge
County: Albert, New Brunswick
Township: Coverdale

GPS Position: 46°02'37.1"N 64°52'41.1"W
Directions: From Cloverdale, head east on Coverdale Rd/NB-112 E for 1.0 km and turn right onto Mitton Rd and the bridge
Crosses: Branch of Turtle Creek
Carries: Mitton Road
Builder: Not known
Year Built: Not known (M1942)
Truss Type: Burr
Dimensions: 1 span, 26 meters, 85 feet
Notes: The bridge was originally in Kent County, although the site and build date are not known. It is currently in very poor condition.

World Index Number: NB/55-01-22
National Register of Historic Places: Not listed

Ellis Covered Bridge (North Becaguimec River #4)
County: Carleton, New Brunswick
Township: Brighton

GPS Position: 46°21'12.6"N 67°23'12.5"W
Directions: From Carlisle, head northwest on Rte 104 N/NB-104 N for 0.4 km and keep right to continue on Howard Brook Rd and after 0.5 km turn right onto Ellis Rd to find the bridge
Crosses: North branch of the Becaguimec River
Carries: Ellis Road
Builder: W.R. Fawcett
Year Built: 2909
Truss Type: Howe and Queen
Dimensions: 1 span, 19 meters, 63 feet
Notes: Found in a pleasant rural setting, the structure has been bypassed. It seems to be in good shape.

World Index Number: NB/55-02-05
National Register of Historic Places: Not listed

Florenceville Covered Bridge
County: Carleton, New Brunswick
Township: Florenceville

GPS Position: 46°26'30.1"N 67°37'16.7"W
Directions: In the town of Florenceville, the bridge is found on Old Florenceville Bridge Road, just off of NB-105
Crosses: St John River
Carries: Old Florenceville Bridge Road
Builder: Not known
Year Built: 1910
Truss Type: Howe
Dimensions: 1 span, 47 meters, 154 feet
Notes: The original bridge was uncovered and opened in 1885. Subsequently the western portion was covered using a Howe Truss, and later the east span was covered. It is a terrific looking bridge.
World Index Number: NB/55-02-06
National Register of Historic Places: March 31, 2009

Hartland Covered Bridge
County: Carleton, New Brunswick
Township: Hartland

GPS Position: 46°17'48.1"N 67°31'49.1"W
Directions: In the town of Hartland, the bridge is found on the Hartland Hill Bridge Road crossing the St. John River, just off NB-105
Crosses: St. John River
Carries: Hartland Hill Bridge Road
Builder: Hartland Bridge Company
Year Built: 1901
Truss Type: Howe
Dimensions: 7 spans, 392 meters, 1282 feet
Notes: This is the world's longest covered bridge and a magnificent structure. You can read more about it on page 21.
World Index Number: NB/55-02-07
National Register of Historic Places: June 23, 1980

Benton Covered Bridge (Eel River #3)
County: Carleton and York, New Brunswick
Township: Benton

GPS Position: 45°59'12.1"N 67°36'29.9"W
Directions: From Oak Mountain, head south on Oak Mountain Rd/Squires Mill Rd for 0.5 km and continue on Squires Mill Rd for 3.9 km. to Benton Rd where you find the bridge
Crosses: Eel River
Carries: Benton Road
Builder: Not known
Year Built: 1927
Truss Type: Howe and Queen
Dimensions: 1 span, 33 meters, 107 feet
Notes: The Benton Covered Bridge is in a pleasant rural area with a small park and picnic tables and surrounded by hay fields.
World Index Number: NB/55-02-15 / NB-15-12
National Register of Historic Places: Not listed

Canal Covered Bridge
County: Charlotte, New Brunswick
Township: St. George

GPS Position: 45°09'36.7"N 66°49'38.3"W
Directions: In the town of Canal, head north on Canal Road off of Maxwell Road and the bridge is 0.2 km.
Crosses: Canal Stream
Carries: Canal Road

Builder: Not known
Year Built: 1917
Truss Type: Howe and Queen
Dimensions: 1 span, 38 meters, 124 feet
Notes: The Canal Stream is a natural canal which connects Lake Utopia to the Bay of Fundy. It helps provide the site with a tranquil atmosphere
World Index Number: NB/55-03-01
National Register of Historic Places: Not listed

Dumbarton CB (Digdeguash River #6)
County: Charlotte, New Brunswick
Township: Dumbarton

GPS Position: 45°22'42.6"N 67°07'49.8"W
Directions: From Dumbarton, head northeast on Tryon Rd
toward St Andrews Trail for 0.2 km and you will find the bridge
Crosses: Digdeguash River
Carries: St Andrews Trail

Builder: **Not known**
Year Built: 1928
Truss Type: Howe
Dimensions: 1 span, 23 meters, 75 feet
Notes: The bridge is unpainted and without windows, which is
not unusual for New Brunswick bridges. It is in a quiet setting

World Index Number: NB/55-03-02
National Register of Historic Places: Not listed

Flume Ridge CB (Magaguadavic River #7)
County: Charlotte, New Brunswick
Township: Dumbarton

GPS Position: 45°27'25.2"N 67°00'58.3"W
Directions: From the village of Flume Ridge, head southeast on Flume Ridge Rd for 4.3 km and turn left onto Mill Rd where the bridge is 1.0 km
Crosses: Magaguadavic River
Carries: Mill Road
Builder: Not known
Year Built: 1905
Truss Type: Modified Pratt and Queen
Dimensions: 1 span, 19 meters, 62 feet
Notes: The bridge is located in a remote area but easy to drive to and worth the effort.

World Index Number: NB/55-03-03
National Register of Historic Places: Not listed

Maxwell Crossing CB (Dennis Stream #3)
County: Charlotte, New Brunswick
Township: St. Stephen

GPS Position: 45°14'41.3"N 67°16'00.5"W
Directions: From the village of Maxwell Crossing, head southwest on Maxwell Crossing Rd for 0.3 km and the bridge
Crosses: Dennis Stream
Carries: Maxwell Crossing Road
Builder: Frank L. Boone
Year Built: 1910 (R2013)
Truss Type: Howe
Dimensions: 1 span, 20 meters, 64 feet
Notes: In January of 2013, the structure was badly damaged by a vehicle and was being considered for demolition. However it was repaired and opened again for traffic

World Index Number: NB/55-03-04
National Register of Historic Places: Not listed

McGuire CB (Dyer, Digdeguash River #3)
County: Charlotte, New Brunswick
Township: St. Patrick

GPS Position: 45°15'24.8"N 67°00'21.3"W
Directions: From the village of Saint Patrick, head northwest on NB-760 W for 0.9 km and see the bridge
Crosses: Digdeguash River
Carries: NB-760 W
Builder: Not known
Year Built: 1915 (R2017)
Truss Type: Howe
Dimensions: 1 span, 37 meters, 118 feet
Notes: The bridge was closed in 2013 and being considered for replacement by a modern bridge. Local residents have objected and in 2017 the government agreed to repair it

World Index Number: NB/55-03-05
National Register of Historic Places: Not listed

Mill Pond CB (Hanson Mill Pond, Little Lepreau River #1.5)
County: Charlotte, New Brunswick
Township: Lepreau

GPS Position: 45°08'04.0"N 66°27'37.1"W
Directions: From the village of Little Lepreau, head west on Little Lepreau Rd for 0.3 km and the bridge is on the right
Crosses: Little Lepreau River
Carries: Little Lepreau Road (Bypassed)
Builder: Not Known
Year Built: 1910 (M1986)
Truss Type: Howe
Dimensions: 1 span, 33 meters, 107 feet
Notes: The bridge is no longer in service after being moved in 1986. It is well worth a visit though.

World Index Number: NB/55-03-06
National Register of Historic Places: Not listed

McCann Covered Bridge (Digdeguash River #4)
County: Charlotte, New Brunswick
Township: Dumbarton

GPS Position: 45°18'47.8"N 67°04'19.7"W
Directions: From the town of Rollingdam, head northeast on NB-770 S for 0.5 km to find the bridge
Crosses: Digdeguash River
Carries: NB-770 S

Builder: Not known
Year Built: 1938
Truss Type: Howe
Dimensions: 1 span, 27 meters, 89 feet
Notes: A beautiful bridge in a nice location. The awning window is a nice detail.

World Index Number: NB/55-03-09
National Register of Historic Places: Not listed

Village Historique Acadien Covered Bridge
County: Gloucester, New Brunswick
Township: Rivière-du-Nord

GPS Position: 47°47'14.6"N 65°06'22.3"W
Directions: 5 Rue du Pont, Bertrand
Crosses: Pond
Carries: Pedestrian walkway

Builder: Not known
Year Built: 2000
Truss Type: Howe and Queen
Dimensions: 1 span, 22 meters, 72 feet
Notes: Located in an exhibit of historical Acadian buildings. There is an admission charge but the whole site is worth a visit.

World Index Number: NB/55-04-11
National Register of Historic Places: Not listed

Tom Graham Covered Bridge
County: Kent, New Brunswick
Township: Weldford

GPS Position: 46°34'36.0"N 64°57'20.2"W
Directions: From the town of Lower Main River, head northeast on NB-510 E for 2.9 km to find the bridge
Crosses: Tom Graham Creek
Carries: NB-510 E

Builder: Not known
Year Built: 1928
Truss Type: Howe and Queen
Dimensions: 1 span, 31 meters, 72 feet
Notes: Found in a tranquil rural setting, the bridge still carries traffic

World Index Number: NB/55-05-03
National Register of Historic Places: Not listed

Camerons Mill CB (Kouchibouguasis River #5)
County: Kent, New Brunswick
Township: St. Louis

GPS Position: 46°40'17.0"N 65°08'19.7"W
Directions: From the town of Camerons Mill, head southwest on Chem. Saint-Ignace Station for 2.0 km and turn right onto Chem. Camerons Mill Cross where the bridge is 0.5 km
Crosses: Tom Graham Creek
Carries: Chem. Camerons Mill Cross

Builder: Not known
Year Built: 1950
Truss Type: Howe and Queen
Dimensions: 1 span, 43 meters, 140 feet
Notes: This bridge is situated in a beautiful tranquil setting

World Index Number: NB/55-05-12
National Register of Historic Places: Not listed

Bloomfield Covered Bridge
County: Kings, New Brunswick
Township: Norton

GPS Position: 45°34'51.2"N 65°45'39.8"W
Directions: From the town of Bloomfield, head northwest on Bloomfield Station Rd for 0.7 km and the bridge
Crosses: Bloomfield Creek
Carries: Bloomfield Station Road

Builder: Not known
Year Built: 1918 (R2013)
Truss Type: Howe and Queen
Dimensions: 1 span, 46 meters, 151 feet
Notes: The bridge still carries vehicles and can be relatively busy. The 2013 repairs were needed due to vehicle damage

World Index Number: NB/55-06-01
National Register of Historic Places: Not listed

Centreville Covered Bridge (Millstream River #5)
County: Kings, New Brunswick
Township: Studholm

GPS Position: 45°48'28.7"N 65°35'39.4"W
Directions: From the town of Pleasant Ridge, head southeast on Pleasant Ridge Branch Rd for 1.7 km and the bridge
Crosses: Millstream River
Carries: Pleasant Ridge Branch Road

Builder: Not known
Year Built: 1911
Truss Type: Howe and Queen
Dimensions: 1 span, 30 meters, 98 feet
Notes: Found in a tranquil rural setting. The bridge still carries traffic, although it is not busy

World Index Number: NB/55-06-02
National Register of Historic Places: Not listed

Darlings Island Covered Bridge
County: Kings, New Brunswick
Township: Hampton

GPS Position: 45°28'51.6"N 65°53'51.5"W
Directions: From the town of Darlings Island, head southwest on Darlings Island Rd for 3.7 km and the bridge
Crosses: Hammond River
Carries: Darlings Island Road (Bypassed)

Builder: Not known
Year Built: 1914
Truss Type: Howe and Queen
Dimensions: 1 span, 23 meters, 140 feet
Notes: The bridge was built to help Darling Island residents to travel to the mainland. The bridge was bypassed in 1996.

World Index Number: NB/55-06-04
National Register of Historic Places: Not listed

Malone Covered Bridge (Kennebecasis River #23)
County: Kings, New Brunswick
Township: Cardwell

GPS Position: 45°45'28.6"N 65°12'10.0"W
Directions: From the town of Upper Goshen, head south on Upper Goshen Rd for 1.5 km and the bridge
Crosses: Kennebecasis River
Carries: Upper Goshen Road

Builder: Not known
Year Built: 1910
Truss Type: Howe
Dimensions: 1 span, 19 meters, 64 feet
Notes: The road in from the highway is a long and rough gravel surface. Use caution, particularly after rain.

World Index Number: NB/55-06-11
National Register of Historic Places: Not listed

Marven Covered Bridge (Belleisle Creek #2)
County: Kings, New Brunswick
Township: Springfield

GPS Position: 45°41'19.8"N 65°46'18.8"W
Directions: From Upper Midland, go NW on Menzies Rd for 0.8 km and turn left onto Swamp Rd and the bridge is 0.3 km
Crosses: Belleisle Creek
Carries: Swamp Road

Builder: Whitman Brewer
Year Built: 1903
Truss Type: Howe and Queen
Dimensions: 1 span, 24 meters, 79 feet
Notes: A nice looking bridge in a quiet setting, the interior has been hit with graffiti.

World Index Number: NB/55-06-12
National Register of Historic Places: Not listed

MacFarlane Covered Bridge (Ward's Creek #2)
County: Kings, New Brunswick
Township: Sussex

GPS Position: 45°39'19.7"N 65°30'45.5"W
Directions: From Sussex, head south on Church Ave for 1.5 km and continue onto Wards Creek Rd and the site is 6.4 km
Crosses: Ward's Creek
Carries: Wards Creek Road

Builder: A.E. Smye
Year Built: 1909
Truss Type: Howe
Dimensions: 1 span, 19 meters, 63 feet
Notes: This bridge has had a recent rehabilitation and looks excellent in a natural setting

World Index Number: NB/55-06-13
National Register of Historic Places: Not listed

Bayswater Covered Bridge (Milkish Inlet #1)
County: Kings, New Brunswick
Township: Westfield

GPS Position: 45°21'17.9"N 66°07'53.3"W
Directions: From Bayswater, head go northeast on NB-845 for a short distance and see the bridge
Crosses: Milkish Inlet
Carries: NB-845

Builder: Not known
Year Built: 1920 (R2021)
Truss Type: Howe and Queen
Dimensions: 2 spans, 67 meters, 218 feet
Notes: A major repair at a cost of over a million dollars was completed in 2021

World Index Number: NB/55-06-15
National Register of Historic Places: Not listed

Moores Mills CB (Waterford, Trout Creek #5)
County: Kings, New Brunswick
Township: Waterford

GPS Position: 45°40'56.5"N 65°22'20.6"W
Directions: From Waterford, head northwest on Waterford Rd for 0.2 km and turn right onto Drummond Rd and the bridge
Crosses: Trout Creek
Carries: Drummond Road

Builder: Not known
Year Built: 1923
Truss Type: Howe and Queen
Dimensions: 1 span, 19 meters, 64 feet
Notes: The bridge is located close to Fundy National Park and is in a beautiful natural setting

World Index Number: NB/55-06-16
National Register of Historic Places: Not listed

Oldfields Covered Bridge (Smith Creek #5)
County: Kings, New Brunswick
Township: Studholm

GPS Position: 45°49'47.8"N 65°26'39.2"W
Directions: From the town of Newtown, head south on Oldfield Rd for 0.3 km and you will find the bridge
Crosses: Smith Creek
Carries: Oldfield Road

Builder: Not known
Year Built: 1920
Truss Type: Howe
Dimensions: 1 span, 30 meters, 98 feet
Notes: This bridge was featured on a 1992 Canadian quarter. It is in a great setting

World Index Number: NB/55-06-17
National Register of Historic Places: Not listed

Plumweseep CB (Kennebecasis River)
County: Kings, New Brunswick
Township: Sussex

GPS Position: 45°44'29.0"N 65°26'48.2"W
Directions: From the town of Plumweseep, head south on Plumweseep Rd for 1.4 km and see the bridge
Crosses: Kennebecasis River
Carries: Plumweseep Road
Builder: Albert E. Smye
Year Built: 1910 (R2018)
Truss Type: Howe and Queen
Dimensions: 1 span, 22 meters, 78 feet
Notes: The bridge is named for the indigenous word for Salmon River. The 2013 repairs were necessitated by damage from a vehicle.

World Index Number: NB/55-06-18
National Register of Historic Places: Not listed

Urney Covered Bridge (Picadilly, Trout Creek #4)
County: Kings, New Brunswick
Township: Waterford

GPS Position: 45°41'34.2"N 65°23'52.5"W
Directions: From Waterford, head NW on Waterford Rd for 2.7 km and turn right onto Urney Rd and the bridge is 0.2 km
Crosses: Trout Creek
Carries: Urney Road

Builder: Whitman Brewer
Year Built: 1908
Truss Type: Howe and Queen
Dimensions: 1` span, 20 meters, 968 feet
Notes: The bridge is still in service, primarily by local residents. There is a popular hiking trail nearby

World Index Number: NB/55-06-19
National Register of Historic Places: Not listed

Salmon CB (Kennebecasis River #7.5)
County: Kings, New Brunswick
Township: Sussex

GPS Position: 45°44'42.8"N 65°29'53.1"W
Directions: From Sussex, head north on Smiths Creek Rd/NB-890 E from NB-1 for 1.0 km and find the bridge
Crosses: Kennebecasis River
Carries: Smiths Creek Road (Bypassed)

Builder: W.R. Fawcett
Year Built: 1907
Truss Type: Howe
Dimensions: 1 span, 36 meters, 119 feet
Notes: The bridge is closed to traffic and has been bypassed. It has a roadside park at the site

World Index Number: NB/55-06-21
National Register of Historic Places: Not listed

Smithtown Covered Bridge (Hammond River #3)
County: Kings, New Brunswick
Township: Hampton

GPS Position: 45°27'49.6"N 65°48'18.7"W
Directions: From the village of Damascus, head northwest on Damascus Rd for 0.3 km and find the bridge
Crosses: Hammond River
Carries: Damascus Road

Builder: Not known
Year Built: 1914 (R2022)
Truss Type: Howe and Queen
Dimensions: 1 span, 57 meters, 187 feet
Notes: During the recent repairs, the scaffolding collapsed into the river due to high water. The bridge looks great now.

World Index Number: NB/55-06-24
National Register of Historic Places: Not listed

Tranton Covered Bridge (Smith Creek #1)
County: Kings, New Brunswick
Township: Sussex

GPS Position: 45°44'52.0"N 65°30'44.0"W
Directions: From Roachville, head north on McGregor Brook Rd from NB-10 and continue onto Roachville Rd and the bridge is 2.8 km
Crosses: Smith Creek
Carries: Roachville Road
Builder: Not known
Year Built: 1925
Truss Type: Howe and Queen
Dimensions: 1 span, 39 meters, 127 feet
Notes: Found in a beautiful rural setting, the bridge still carries vehicle traffic

World Index Number: NB/55-06-26
National Register of Historic Places: Not listed

Moosehorn CB (Moosehorn Creek #1.5)
County: Kings, New Brunswick
Township: Norton

GPS Position: 45°36'33.0"N 65°43'14.8"W
Directions: From the town of Bloomfield, head northeast on New Brunswick Route 1 E/NB-1 E for 4.7 km and find the bridge
Crosses: Moosehorn Creek
Carries: NB-1
Builder: Not known
Year Built: 1915
Truss Type: Howe and Queen
Dimensions: 1 span, 30 meters, 98 feet
Notes: The bridge is located by the busy NB-1. It was bypassed and closed to vehicle traffic

World Index Number: NB/55-06-29
National Register of Historic Places: Not listed

Boniface Covered Bridge (Green River #3)
County: Madawaska, New Brunswick
Township: Saint-Basile

GPS Position: 47°22'17.3"N 68°09'07.3"W
Directions: From Saint-Basile, head NE on Chemin Mgr Lang for 2.3 km and continue straight onto Rang 3. After 5.8 km turn right onto Chem. Davis and in 0.5 km, left onto Chem. Boniface where the bridge is 0.3 km
Crosses: Greeen River
Carries: Chem. Boniface
Builder: Not known
Year Built: 1925
Truss Type: Howe
Dimensions: 2 spans, 59 meters, 194 feet
Notes: This bridge still carries traffic. It is in a pleasant setting

World Index Number: NB/55-07-02
National Register of Historic Places: Not listed

Morneault Settlement CB (Baker Brook #2)
County: Madawaska, New Brunswick
Township: Baker Brook

GPS Position: 47°20'18.4"N 68°32'56.8"W
Directions: From Concession-de-Baker-Brook, head south on Chem. Joseph Morneault for 1.0 km to see the bridge
Crosses: Baker Brook
Carries: Chem. Joseph Morneault

Builder: Not known
Year Built: 1939
Truss Type: Howe and Queen
Dimensions: 1 span, 20 meters, 98 feet
Notes: The bridge was closed and bypassed in 2004. It looks to be in reasonably good condition.

World Index Number: NB/55-07-04
National Register of Historic Places: Not listed

Quisibis River #2 Covered Bridge
County: Madawaska, New Brunswick
Township: Saint-Anne

GPS Position: 47°18'18.1"N 68°03'30.4"W
Directions: From Prime, head NW on Chem. Lavoie for 4.0 km and turn right onto Chem. Deschênes where the bridge is 0.3 km
Crosses: Quisibis River
Carries: Chem. Deschênes
Builder: Not known
Year Built: 1952
Truss Type: Howe
Dimensions: 1 span, 20 meters, 63 feet
Notes: The bridge was closed and bypassed in 2019 after being damaged by flood the previous year. .

World Index Number: NB/55-07-05
National Register of Historic Places: Not listed

Nelson Hollow Covered Bridge (Mill Brook #0.5)
County: Northumberland, New Brunswick
Township: Ludlow

GPS Position: 46°32'19.4"N 66°11'12.7"W
Directions: From Amostown, head northeast on NB-8 N for 0.7 k and turn left onto Lyons Ln where the bridge is 0.8 km
Crosses: Betts Mill Brook
Carries: Lyons Lane

Builder: Not known
Year Built: 1899
Truss Type: Howe and Queen
Dimensions: 1 span, 23 meters, 78 feet
Notes: This is the oldest surviving Covered Bridge in New Brunswick.

World Index Number: NB/55-08-08
National Register of Historic Places: Not listed

Burpee Covered Bridge (Gaspereau River #2)
County: Queens, New Brunswick
Township: Ludlow

GPS Position: 46°16'51.0"N 65°51'40.3"W
Directions: From Gaspereau Forks, head northwest on NB-123 N for 4.9 km and turn right on East Gaspereau Rd where the bridge is 0.1 km
Crosses: Gaspereau River
Carries: East Gaspereau Road
Builder: Not known
Year Built: 1912
Truss Type: Howe and Queen
Dimensions: 1 span, 51 meters, 168 feet
Notes: The bridge is open to vehicle traffic and looks to be in good condition

World Index Number: NB/55-09-01
National Register of Historic Places: Not listed

Starkey Covered Bridge (Long Creek #1)
County: Queens, New Brunswick
Township: Chipman

GPS Position: 45°54'03.4"N 65°48'11.3"W
Directions: From Long Creek, head northeast on Starkey Rd for 1.6 km and turn right onto NB-10 E and the site is 2.2 km
Crosses: Long Creek
Carries: NB-10 E

Builder: Dan Starkey
Year Built: 1939
Truss Type: Howe and Queen
Dimensions: 1 span, 42 meters, 139 feet
Notes: The bridge was closed in 2018 due to flood damage but has recently been re-opened

World Index Number: NB/55-09-08
National Register of Historic Places: Not listed

Tynemouth Creek Covered Bridge
County: Saint John, New Brunswick
Township: Simonds

GPS Position: 45°18'04.6"N 65°39'25.7"W
Directions: From Tynemouth Creek, head northwest on Tynemouth Creek Rd and the bridge is a short distance
Crosses: Tynemouth Creek
Carries: Tynemouth Creek Road

Builder: Not known
Year Built: 1927
Truss Type: Howe
Dimensions: 1 span 31 meters, 103 feet
Notes: Tynemouth Creek is a tidal river, and with the right timing you can get good side images

World Index Number: NB/55-11-04
National Register of Historic Places: Not listed

Hardscrabble CB (Irish River#2, Vaughan Creek#2)
County: Saint John, New Brunswick
Township: St Martins

GPS Position: 45°21'33.1"N 65°32'11.7"W
Directions: From St. Martins, head NW on Main St for 1.7 km and turn left onto Vaughan Ln where the bridge is 0.3 km
Crosses: Vaughan Creek
Carries: Vaughan Lane
Builder: Not known
Year Built: 1946 (R1996)
Truss Type: Howe
Dimensions: 1 span, 24 meters, 78 feet
Notes: A pedestrian walkway was added in 1996. It also has two vehicle lanes, usually known as double-barrelled

World Index Number: NB/55-11-06
National Register of Historic Places: Not listed

Irish River #1 Covered Bridge (Vaughan Creek)
County: Saint John, New Brunswick
Township: St Martins

GPS Position: 45°21'32.0"N 65°31'55.9"W
Directions: From St. Martins, head NW on Main St for 2.2 km
and turn right onto Big Salmon River Rd to find the bridge
Crosses: Vaughan Creek
Carries: Big Salmon River Road
Builder: Not known
Year Built: 2022
Truss Type: Multiple Kingpost
Dimensions: 1 span, 24 meters, 78 feet
Notes: The original 1935 bridge was demolished with plans to
build a modern bridge. Local pressure persuaded the building
of this new covered bridge

World Index Number: NB/55-11-05#2
National Register of Historic Places: Not listed

Hoyt Station Covered Bridge (Back Creek #2)
County: Sunbury, New Brunswick
Township: Blissville

GPS Position: 45°34'26.8"N 66°32'20.0"W
Directions: From the town of Hoyt, head SW on NB-101 S for 1.7 km and turn left onto Hoyt Station Rd to find the bridge
Crosses: Back Creek
Carries: Hoyt Station Road

Builder: Not known
Year Built: 1909
Truss Type: Howe and Queen
Dimensions: 1 span, 20 meters, 67 feet
Notes: The trees offer a nice background to the structure

World Index Number: NB/55-12-02
National Register of Historic Places: Not listed

Smythe (Mill Settlement, South Oromocto River #2)
County: Sunbury, New Brunswick
Township: Blissville

GPS Position: 45°34'22.6"N 66°34'44.9"W
Directions: From the town of Hoyt, head SE on Mill Settlement Rd for 2.2 km and turn right onto N Mill Settlement Rd and the site is 0.2 km
Crosses: South Branch of the Oromocto River
Carries: N Mill Settlement Road
Builder: Not known
Year Built: 1915
Truss Type: Howe and Queen
Dimensions: 1 span, 42 meters, 139 feet
Notes: This tranquil rural site offers multiple excellent views for photographers
World Index Number: NB/55-12-03
National Register of Historic Places: Not listed

Patrick Owens CB (Rusagonis River #2)
County: Sunbury, New Brunswick
Township: Rusagonis

GPS Position: 45°48'13.7"N 66°37'10.9"W
Directions: From the town of Rusagonis, head northeast on Wilsey Rd for 0.1 km and you will find the bridge
Crosses: Rusagonis River
Carries: Wilsey Road

Builder: McLaggen and Boone
Year Built: 1909
Truss Type: Howe and Queen
Dimensions: 2 spans, 72 meters, 236 feet
Notes: In a pleasant rural setting, it has an interesting full length window on one side

World Index Number: NB/55-12-05
National Register of Historic Places: Not listed

Tomlinson Mill CB (Odellach River #2)
County: Victoria, New Brunswick
Township: Gordon

GPS Position: 46°46'48.6"N 67°29'46.2"W
Directions: From the town of Licford, head south on Tomlinson Mill Rd off NB-109 for 0.7 km and see the bridge
Crosses: Odellach River
Carries: Tomlinson Mill Road

Builder: Not known
Year Built: 1918
Truss Type: Howe
Dimensions: 1 span, 20 meters, 64 feet
Notes: This is the last surviving covered bridge in Victoria County. It is open to vehicle traffic.

World Index Number: NB/55-13-03
National Register of Historic Places: Not listed

Budd Covered Bridge (Cocagne River #5)
County: Westmoreland, New Brunswick
Township: Moncton

GPS Position: 46°14'23.4"N 64°53'14.4"W
Directions: From New Scotland, head northeast on New Scotland Rd for 3.9 km and turn right onto Victoria Rd where the bridge is 2.2 km
Crosses: Cocagne River
Carries: Victoria Road
Builder: Not known
Year Built: 1912
Truss Type: Howe and Queen
Dimensions: 1 span, 27 meters, 86 feet
Notes: This bridge continues to service vehicle traffic. It is one of the seven covered bridges in the county.

World Index Number: NB/55-14-05
National Register of Historic Places: Not listed

Joshua Gallant CB (Shediac River #4)
County: Westmorland, New Brunswick
Township: Shediac

GPS Position: 46°14'42.0"N 64°39'52.2"W
Directions: From the town of Evangeline, head east on Shediac River Rd for 3.2 km where you find the bridge
Crosses: Shediac River
Carries: Shediac River Road

Builder: Not known
Year Built: 1935
Truss Type: Howe and Queen
Dimensions: 1 span, 27 meters, 86 feet
Notes: While this bridge is closed to automobile traffic, it is part of the province's snowmobile trail system

World Index Number: NB/55-14-07
National Register of Historic Places: Not listed

Boudreau CB (Gayton, Memramcook River)
County: Westmorland, New Brunswick
Township: Dorchester

GPS Position: 46°01'36.0"N 64°33'51.0"W
Directions: From Memramcook, head north on Rue Renaissance Ext St/Royal Rd for 2.4 km and turn left onto Gayton Rd and the bridge is 0.5 km
Crosses: Memramcook River
Carries: Gayton Road
Builder: Not known
Year Built: 1930
Truss Type: Howe and Queen
Dimensions: 1 span, 23 meters, 78 feet
Notes: One of the few of the province's Covered Bridges which is listed as a Historic Place. It is open to traffic.

World Index Number: NB/55-14-08
National Register of Historic Places: November 3, 2009

Hasty Covered Bridge (Petitcodiac River #3)
County: Westmorland, New Brunswick
Township: River Glade

GPS Position: 45°59'51.6"N 65°05'27.0"W
Directions: From River Glade, head NW on NB-106 E for 1.6 km and turn right onto Salisbury Rd/NB-106 E. In 1.0 km turn right onto Powers Pit Rd where the site is 0.6 km
Crosses: Petitcodiac River
Carries: Powers Pit Road
Builder: Not known
Year Built: 1931 (R2016)
Truss Type: Howe
Dimensions: 1 span, 38 meters, 126 feet
Notes: This is a popular spot for canoes and kayaks and their is a boat launch at one end of the bridge

World Index Number: NB/55-14-09
National Register of Historic Places: Not listed

Poirier Covered Bridge (Cocagne River #3)
County: Westmorland, New Brunswick
Township: Moncton

GPS Position: 46°16'07.8"N 64°47'48.0"W
Directions: From the town of Poirier, head southeast on Poirier Office Rd for 1.0 km and find the bridge
Crosses: Cocagne River
Carries: Poirier Office Road

Builder: Not known
Year Built: 1942
Truss Type: Howe and Queen
Dimensions: 1 span, 45 meters, 142 feet
Notes: Located north of the city of Moncton, the bridge still carries vehicle traffic

World Index Number: NB/55-14-12
National Register of Historic Places: Not listed

Wheaton Covered Bridge (Tantramar River #2)
County: Westmorland, New Brunswick
Township: Sackville

GPS Position: 45°55'54.6"N 64°19'49.8"W
Directions: From Middle Sackville, head SW on Church St for 0.2 km, then turn left to stay on Church St. After 1.1 km turn right on High Marsh Rd and the site is 1.1 km
Crosses: Tantramar River
Carries: High Marsh Rd
Builder: Not known
Year Built: 1916 (R1990)
Truss Type: Howe and Queen
Dimensions: 1 span, 51 meters, 165 feet
Notes: Steel supports were added in the 1990 repairs. The structure looks in excellent condition and open to traffic

World Index Number: NB/55-14-13
National Register of Historic Places: Not listed

Parkindale Covered Bridge (Magnetic Hill)
County: Westmorland, New Brunswick
Township: Moncton

GPS Position: 46°08'09.6"N 64°53'18.0"W
Directions: From Moncton, head NW on Mountain Rd for 0.5 km and turn right onto Magic Mountain Rd to find the bridge
Crosses: brook
Carries: Magic Mountain Road

Builder: Not known
Year Built: 1916 (M1982)
Truss Type: Howe and Queen
Dimensions: 1 span, 17 meters, 57 feet
Notes: The bridge was moved to the Magnetic Hill Game Park in 1982 from an Albert County site. Admission charge

World Index Number: NB/55-14-14
National Register of Historic Places: Not listed

Nackawic Siding CB (Nackawic Stream #5)
County: York, New Brunswick
Township: Southampton

GPS Position: 46°08'45.0"N 67°16'36.0"W
Directions: From the town of Woodman, head west on Nackawic Siding Rd for 0.4 km and find the bridge
Crosses: Nackawic River
Carries: Nackawic Siding Road

Builder: Not known
Year Built: 1927
Truss Type: Howe and Queen
Dimensions: 1 span, 20 meters, 65 feet
Notes: Use caution on the Nackawic Siding Road as it can be rough, particularly after wet weather

World Index Number: NB/55-15-06
National Register of Historic Places: Not listed

New Brunswick Tours

The following tours are designed to visit multiple bridges in an efficient manner

Albert County Tour

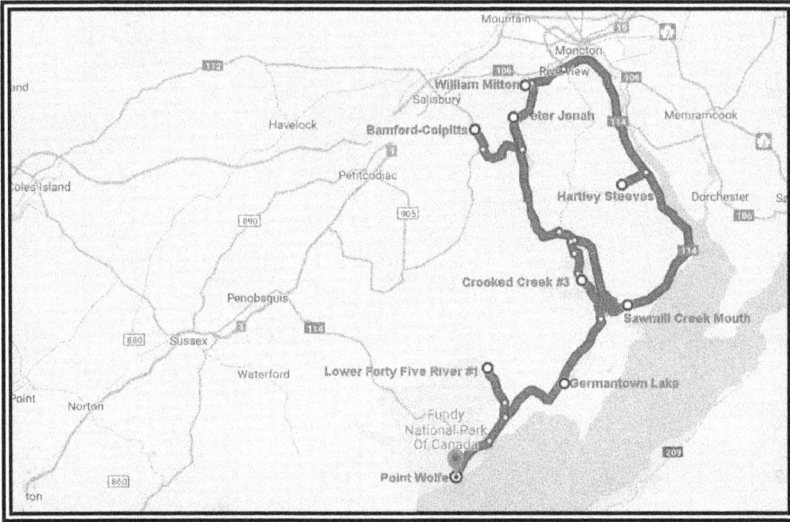

9 Bridges- 3.5 hours driving

Bamford-Colpitts	45°59'18.0"N 64°58'25.6"W
Peter Jonah	46°00'10.4"N 64°54'00.7"W
William Mitton	46°02'37.1"N 64°52'41.1"W
Hartley Steeves	45°55'01.9"N 64°42'03.6"W
Sawmill Creek Mouth	45°45'52.9"N 64°41'33.0"W
Crooked Creek #3	45°47'49.2"N 64°46'36.1"W
Lower Forty Five River #1	45°41'13.2"N 64°57'10.8"W
Germantown Lake	45°40'00.1"N 64°48'40.7"W
Point Wolfe	45°33'02.5"N 65°00'46.8"W

Carleton and York Counties Tour

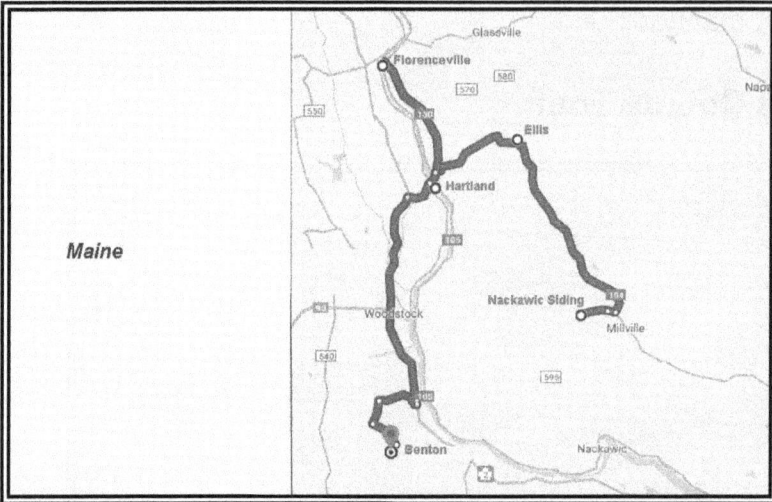

5 Bridges- 2 hrs driving

Nackawic Siding	46°08'45.0"N 67°16'36.0"W
Ellis	46°21'12.6"N 67°23'12.5"W
Hartland	46°17'48.1"N 67°31'49.1"W
Florenceville	46°26'30.1"N 67°37'16.7"W
Benton	45°59'12.1"N 67°36'29.9"W

Note: The road into Nackawic Siding Covered Bridge can be rough and a high clearance vehicle is recommended. It is particularly bad if their has been recent rain.

Charlotte County Tour

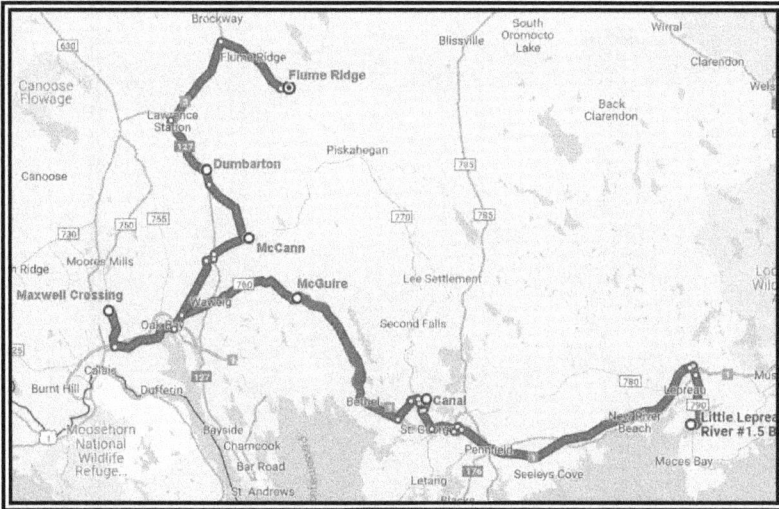

7 Bridges- 2 hours 15 min

Mill Pond	45°08'04.0"N 66°27'37.1"W
Canal	45°09'36.7"N 66°49'38.3"W
McGuire	45°15'24.8"N 67°00'21.3"W
Maxwell Crossing	45°14'41.3"N 67°16'00.5"W
McCann	45°18'47.8"N 67°04'19.7"W
Dumbarton	45°22'42.6"N 67°07'49.8"W
Flume Ridge	45°27'25.2"N 67°00'58.3"W

Kings County East Tour

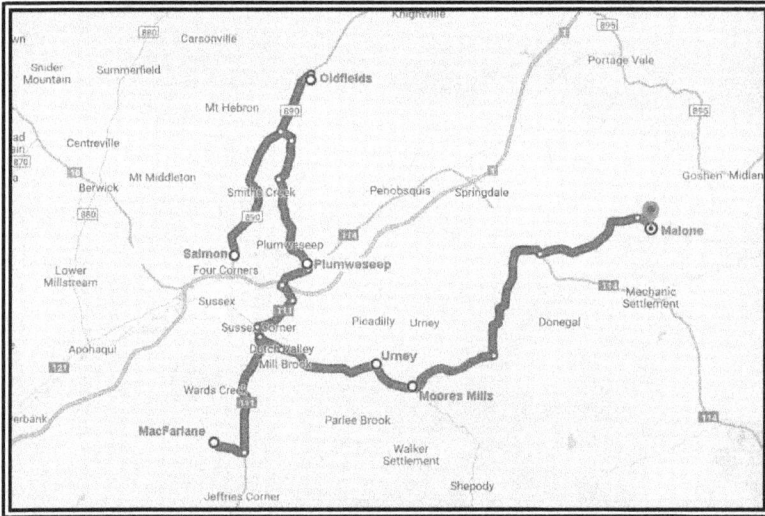

7 Bridges- 1 hr 30 min driving

Salmon	45°44'42.8"N 65°29'53.1"W
Oldfields	45°49'47.8"N 65°26'39.2"W
Plumweseep	45°44'29.0"N 65°26'48.2"W
MacFarlane	45°39'19.7"N 65°30'45.5"W
Urney	45°41'34.2"N 65°23'52.5"W
Moores Mills	45°40'56.5"N 65°22'20.6"W
Malone	45°45'28.6"N 65°12'10.0"W

Kings County West Tour

8 Bridges- 2 hrs 15 min driving

Bayswater	45°21'17.9"N 66°07'53.3"W
Darlings Island	45°28'51.6"N 65°53'51.5"W
Smithtown	45°27'49.6"N 65°48'18.7"W
Bloomfield	45°34'51.2"N 65°45'39.8"W
Moosehorn	45°36'33.0"N 65°43'14.8"W
Marven	45°41'19.8"N 65°46'18.8"W
Centreville	45°48'28.7"N 65°35'39.4"W
Tranton	45°44'52.0"N 65°30'44.0"W

Westmoreland County Tour

7 Bridges- 2 hrs driving

Hasty	45°59'51.6"N 65°05'27.0"W
Parkindale	46°08'09.6"N 64°53'18.0"W
Budd	46°14'23.4"N 64°53'14.4"W
Poirier	46°16'07.8"N 64°47'48.0"W
Joshua Gallant	46°14'42.0"N 64°39'52.2"W
Boudreau	46°01'36.0"N 64°33'51.0"W
Wheaton	45°55'54.6"N 64°19'49.8"W

Ontario County Map

West Montrose (Kissing) Covered Bridge
County: Waterloo, Ontario
Township: West Montrose

GPS Position: 43°35'08.1"N 80°28'53.2"W
Directions: From Elmira, head east on Church St E/Waterloo Regional Rd 86 for 6.2 km and turn right onto Covered Bridge Dr and the bridge is 800 m
Crosses: Grand River
Carries: Covered Bridge Dr
Builder: John and Benjamin Bear
Year Built: 1881 (R1933) (R1955) (R1959) (R2000) (R2013)
Truss Type: Howe
Dimensions: 2 Spans, 58 meters, 190 feet
Notes: A major restoration was completed in 2000 by Theo Vandenberk Contracting. It included replacing deteriorated truss members and panels.

World Index Number: ON/59-50-01
National Register of Historic Places: 28 November 2007

York Road Park Covered Bridge
County: Wellington, Ontario
Township: Guelph

GPS Position: 43°32'24.0"N 80°14'29.4"W
Directions: Head southeast on Gordon St from Highway 7 for 230 m and turn left in parking lot and the bridge
Crosses: Speed River
Carries: Pedestrian walkway

Builder: Volunteers
Year Built: 1992
Truss Type: Town
Dimensions: 1 Span, 45 meters, 147 feet

Notes: Opened as part of their trail system and built by volunteers in 1992

World Index Number: ON/59-52-01
National Register of Historic Places: Not listed

Quebec Regional Map

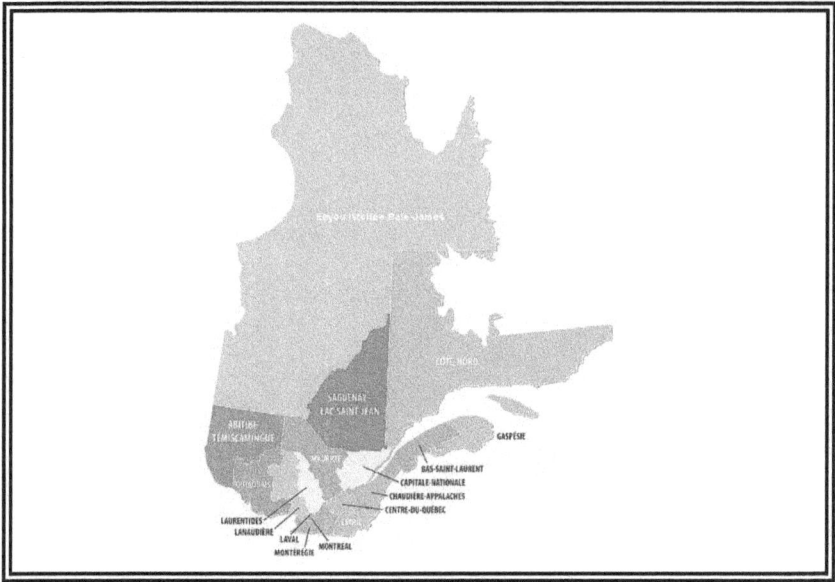

Pont Alphonse-Normandin
Region: Abitibi-Témiscamingue, Québec
Township: Béarn

GPS Position: 48°44'04.0"N 78°09'49.0"W
Directions: From Saint-Dominique-du-Rosaire, head south on Rue Principale for 1.0 km and turn right on QC-109 S. After 2.5 km, turn right on Chem. Lavoie O and the bridge is 3.6 km
Crosses: Riviére Davy
Carries: Chem. Lavoie O
Builder: Ministry of Colonization
Year Built: 1950 (R2013)
Truss Type: Town variation
Dimensions: 1 Span, 40 meters (129 feet)
Notes: The bridge was originally built with arched portals but was changed to angled at some point. It was restored in 2013 when metal beams were added, increasing the load limit.

World Index Number: QC/61-01-05
Formerly Listed in County: Abiti-Est

Pont de l'Orignal
Region: Abitibi-Témiscamingue, Québec
Township: La Morandiére

GPS Position: 48°42'17.0"N 77°33'14.0"W
Directions: From Rochebaucourt, head north on QC-397 N toward for 3.1 km and turn left onto QC-395 S where the bridge is 3.9 km
Crosses: Riviére Laflamme
Carries: QC-395 S
Builder: Ministry of Colonization
Year Built: 1942 (R2002)
Truss Type: Town variation
Dimensions: 1 Span, 37 meters, 118 feet
Notes: The portal was changed from an arch to angled in 2002. The work was done due to flood damage. In English, the name would be Moose Bridge.

World Index Number: QC/61-01-18
Formerly Listed in County: Abiti-Est

Pont Émery-Sicard
Region: Abitibi-Témiscamingue, Québec
Township: Dalquier - Duverny

GPS Position: 48°38'36.0"N 78°00'18.0"W
Directions: From Saint-Maurice-de-Dalquier, head west on QC-395 S for 1.3 km and turn right onto CH Des 5 & 6 Rang to find the bridge
Crosses: Riviére Hurricana
Carries: CH Des 5 & 6 Rang
Builder: Ministry of Colonization
Year Built: 1946 (R1962)
Truss Type: Town variation
Dimensions: 1 Span, 66 meters, 217 feet
Notes: A substantial restoration was completed in 1962. The bridge is named for a local sawmill owner who also supplied the wood.

World Index Number: QC/61-01-22
Formerly Listed in County: Abiti-Est

Pont des Chutes
Region: Abitibi-Témiscamingue, Québec
Township: Rochebaucourt

GPS Position: 48°42'17.0"N 77°26'41.0"W
Directions: From Rochebaucourt, head north on QC-397 N for 3.2 km and turn right onto Ch Des 7 & 8 Rang E. After 4.1 km you will find the bridge
Crosses: Riviére Laflamme
Carries: Ch Des 7 & 8 Rang E
Builder: Ministry of Colonization
Year Built: 1954 (R1961) (R1962)
Truss Type: Town variation
Dimensions: 2 Spans, 64 meters, 212 feet
Notes: In 1964 an abutment was washed away in a flood causing the bridge to break in two. It was repaired the same year. It was closed to traffic in 2010.

World Index Number: QC/61-01-25
Formerly Listed in County: Abiti-Est

Pont de l'Arche de Noé
Region: Abitibi-Témiscamingue, Québec
Township: Rochebaucourt

GPS Position: 48°38'46.0"N 77°39'03.0"W
Directions: From La Morandière, head north on QC-397 N for 3.1 km and turn left on 5e-et-6e Rang O, the bridge is 950 m
Crosses: Ruisseau Tourville
Carries: 5e-et-6e Rang O
Builder: Ministry of Colonization
Year Built: 1937 (R1985)
Truss Type: Town variation
Dimensions: 1 Span, 39 meters, 129 feet
Notes: In 1985, a steel support pier was added. It was painted red around that time as well. It was bypassed in 2010. The English translation is Noah's Arc as the bridge is said to float during a flood

World Index Number: QC/61-01-26
Formerly Listed in County: Abiti-Est

Pont Champagne (Vassan)
Region: Abitibi-Témiscamingue, Québec
Township: Vassan

GPS Position: 48°12'53.0"N 77°55'32.0"W
Directions: From Crique-La Corne, head SW on Chem. de Vassan/QC-111 S for 5.3 km and turn right onto Rte du Chanoine-Richard. After 1.6 km, turn left onto Chem. du Pont-Champagne and the bridge
Crosses: Riviére Vassan
Carries: Chem. du Pont-Champagne
Builder: Ministry of Colonization
Year Built: 1941
Truss Type: Town variation
Dimensions: 1 Span, 32 meters, 105 feet
Notes: Formerly gray, it was painted red in the 1980s. In 1989 a metal support pillar was added. The maximum load was reduced to five tonnes in 2023 to protect the structure
World Index Number: QC/61-01-29
Formerly Listed in County: Abiti-Est

Pont Leclerc
Region: Abitibi-Témiscamingue, Québec
Township: La Sarre

GPS Position: 48°50'11.0"N 79°16'33.0"W
Directions: From Bienvenu, head north on Chem. de la
Calamité for 3.8 km. After Chem. de la Calamité turns left and
becomes 8e-et-9e-Rang O/Rang 8 et 9 E, you will find the
bridge in 2.1 km
Crosses: Ruisseau Bouchard
Carries: 8e-et-9e-Rang O
Builder: Ministry of Colonization
Year Built: 1927
Truss Type: Town variation
Dimensions: 1 Span, 25 meters, 81 feet
Notes: This bridge was built on a town truss variation. This
design was modified by the Quebec Ministry of Colonization a

World Index Number: QC/61-02-05
Formerly Listed in County: Abiti-Est

Pont Molesworth
Region: Abitibi-Témiscamingue, Québec
Township: Macamic

GPS Position: 48°44'56.0"N 78°59'39.0"W
Directions: From Macamic, head east on Av. 1e E/Rang 2e-et-3e O for 600 m and see the bridge
Crosses: Riviére Loïs
Carries: Av. 1e E/Rang 2e-et-3e O
Builder: Ministry of Colonization
Year Built: 1930 (R1950) (R1987) (R2017)
Truss Type: Town variation
Dimensions: 2 Spans, 35 meters, 113 feet

Notes: A central pillar was added in 1950 to increase its load capacity. Originally grey, it was repainted red during major renovations performed in 1987 and 2017

World Index Number: QC/61-02-13
Formerly Listed in County: Abiti-Est

Pont du Petit-Quatre
Region: Abitibi-Témiscamingue, Québec
Township: Des Méloizes

GPS Position: 48°54'29.0"N 79°19'35.0"W
Directions: From Abana, head south on QC-111 S for 4.8 km and turn left onto Chem. du Petit-Quatre, the bridge is 1.9 km
Crosses: Riviére Des Méloizes
Carries: Chem. du Petit-Quatre
Builder: Ministry of Colonization
Year Built: Ca.1950 (R1996) (R2012)
Truss Type: Town variation
Dimensions: 1 Span, 32 meters, 105 feet
Notes: This bridge had been beige and was painted red in 1996 and the portals were changed to angled. It was renovated in 2012, when the capacity was reduced to 5 tonnes from 12. Note the fine detail on the side windows

World Index Number: QC/61-02-20
Formerly Listed in County: Abiti-Est

Pont de l'Île
Region: Abitibi-Témiscamingue, Québec
Township: Roquemaure

GPS Position: 48°41'30.0"N 79°24'27.0"W
Directions: From Clerval, head east on 2e-et-3e Rang for 10.7 km and turn right on Rte du 3e-au-4e-Rang. After 1.6 km continue onto Rte de l'Île-Nepawa for 7.4 km. Continue onto Chem. de l'Île-Nepawa for 3.4 km and the bridge is 950 m
Crosses: Arm of Lac Abitibi
Carries: Chem. de l'Île-Nepawa
Builder: Ministry of Colonization
Year Built: 1946 (R1997) (R2012)
Truss Type: Town variation
Dimensions: 2 Spans, 54 meters, 177 feet
Notes: In 1997, steel beams were added under the deck. The bridge underwent renovations in 2012. At that time, the colour was changed from beige to red.
World Index Number: QC/61-02-23
Formerly Listed in County: Abiti-Est

Pont Levasseur
Region: Abitibi-Témiscamingue, Québec
Township: Macamic

GPS Position: 48°50'07.0"N 78°53'22.0"W
Directions: From Authier-Nord, head south on Rue Principale/Rte Principale for 180 m and turn right onto Chem. du Pont-Couvert. The bridge is 2.1 km
Crosses: Riviére Macamic
Carries: Chem. du Pont-Couvert
Builder: Ministry of Colonization
Year Built: 1928 (R1946) (R1985) (R2015) (R2016)
Truss Type: Town variation
Dimensions: 2 Spans, 39 meters, 132 feet
Notes: A central pillar was added in 1946. In 1985 it was renovated. Following renovations in 2015, the load capacity was reduced to 8 tonnes from 12. It was repainted in 2016

World Index Number: QC/61-02-37
Formerly Listed in County: Abiti-Est

Pont Landry
Region: Abitibi-Témiscamingue, Québec
Township: Latulip-Gaboury

GPS Position: 47°23'49.0"N 79°02'50.0"W
Directions: From Latulipe, head south on Rue du Carr S for and continue onto Mnt du 9e Rang. After 2.9 km, turn right onto 9e Rang O and the bridge is 1.1 km
Crosses: Riviére Fraser
Carries: 9e Rang O
Builder: Ministry of Colonization
Year Built: 1932 (R1991)
Truss Type: Town variation
Dimensions: 1 Span, 33 meters, 107 feet

Notes: It was repaired in 1991 and repainted in 2010. In 2007 it was declared an historic monument by the local municipality

World Index Number: QC/61-70-02
Formerly Listed in County: Témiscamingue

Pont Dénommée
Region: Abitibi-Témiscamingue, Québec
Township: Guigues

GPS Position: 47°29'05.0"N 79°24'26.0"W
Directions: From Kirwan, head north on QC-391 N for 2.4 km and turn left onto Rte à Tanguay. After 3.2 km, continue onto Rte du 6e-Rang and the bridge is 1.2 km
Crosses: Riviére à la Loutre
Carries: Rte du 6e-Rang
Builder: Ministry of Colonization
Year Built: 1933
Truss Type: Town variation
Dimensions: 1 Span, 29 meters, 97 feet
Notes: The bridge was lengthened by 10 meters in the 1950s, and was renovated in 1986. It is closed to traffic in the winter since 1975. The load capacity is 10 tonnes.

World Index Number: QC/61-70-04
Formerly Listed in County: Témiscamingue

Pont du College (Quelle Ouest)
Region: Bas-Saint-Laurent, Québec
Township: Ixworth

GPS Position: 47°17'33.0"N 69°57'06.0"W
Directions: From Saint-Onésime, head southeast on Rue de l'Église for 5.1 km and see the bridge
Crosses: Riviére Ouelle
Carries: Rue de l'Église
Builder: Not known
Year Built: 1920 (R2008) (R2017)
Truss Type: Town variation
Dimensions: 1 Span, 25 meters, 81 feet
Notes: The bridge was closed to vehicle traffic in 1978. The 2008 restoration was done using historical methods. The bridge was heavily damaged in February 2017 by a heavy snow load.

World Index Number: QC/61-32-02
Formerly Listed in County: Kamouraska

Pont de la Chute Neigette
Region: Bas-Saint-Laurent, Québec
Township: Neigette

GPS Position: 48°27'05.0"N 68°18'53.0"W
Directions: From Neigette, head northeast on 5 Rang for 3.9 km and turn right to continue for 1.0 km. Turn left onto Ch Du Rang 2 Neigette E and the bridge is 400 m
Crosses: Riviére Neigette
Carries: Ch Du Rang 2 Neigette E
Builder: Not known
Year Built: 1933 (R2017) (M2017)
Truss Type: Town variation
Dimensions: 1 Span, 30 meters, 97 feet
Notes: The bridge is closed in the winter. It was moved to a field after being replaced by a modern bridge in 2017. In 2019, the Neigette Park was opened with picnic tables and parking.

World Index Number: QC/61-58-03
Formerly Listed in County: Rimouski

Pont des Draveurs
Region: Bas-Saint-Laurent, Québec
Township: Macpès

GPS Position: 48°21'50.0"N 68°22'07.0"W
Directions: From Neigette, head south on 1e Rang de Neigette O for 700 m and turn left onto Chem. du Rang-Double. Continue for 7.8 km and turn left onto Chem. du Pont Couvert/Rte du Pont Couvert and you find the bridge.
Crosses: Riviére Neigette
Carries: Rte du Pont Couvert
Builder: Not known
Year Built: 1930 (R1993) (R2000)
Truss Type: Town variation
Dimensions: 1 Span, 29 meters, 94 feet
Notes: The bridge is located in a tranquil country setting. The 1993 repairs were needed after the abutments collapsed in 1991. In 2000 maintenance work included painting.
World Index Number: QC/61-58-04
Formerly Listed in County: Rimouski

Pont Romain-Caron (Sainte-Jean de la Lande)
Region: Bas-Saint-Laurent, Québec
Township: Robinson

GPS Position: 47°23'43.0"N 68°43'13.0"W
Directions: From Lac-Thibeault, head south on Ch. Bellervie for 600 m and the bridge is on the right
Crosses: branche à Gerry
Carries: Ch. Bellervie
Builder: Romain Caron
Year Built: 1940
Truss Type: Town variation
Dimensions: 1 Span, 32 meters, 105 feet
Notes: It was bypassed in 1979 after the roof collapsed under a heavy snow load. A park was set up in the summer of 2013 which includes a sculpture and interpretation panels. The bridge is named for its builder.

World Index Number: QC/61-71-03
Formerly Listed in County: Témiscouata

Pont Balthazar
Region: Cantons de l'Est, Québec
Township: Farnham

GPS Position: 45°16'51.0"N 72°50'07.0"W
Directions: From Adamsville, head west on Chem. Magenta E for 3.8 km and turn right onto Chem. Léger where you will see the bridge
Crosses: Riviére Yamaska
Carries: Chem. Léger
Builder: Not known
Year Built: 1932 (R2002)
Truss Type: Town variation
Dimensions: 1 Span, 27 meters, 88 feet
Notes: The bridge was named for Gustavus Balthazard, who lived in the area and who had approached authorities requesting a bridge be built. In 2002, the bridge was featured as an advertisement on Canada Savings Bonds.
World Index Number: QC/61-11-01
Formerly Listed in County: Brome

Pont Decelles
Region: Cantons de l'Est, Québec
Township: Farnham

GPS Position: 45°16'51.0"N 72°45'43.0"W
Directions: From Adamsville, head east on Rue Choinière for 550 m and continue onto Chem. Choinière. After 1.2 km, turn left onto Chem. Fortin/Rue Fortin to find the bridge
Crosses: Riviére Yamaska
Carries: Chem. Fortin/Rue Fortin
Builder: Not known
Year Built: 1938 (R2007)
Truss Type: Town variation
Dimensions: 1 Span, 32 meters, 106 feet
Notes: Ernest Decelles presented a petition to authorities requesting a bridge and road be built to service the north side of Rivière Yamaska. The bridge was subsequently named after him. It was closed to traffic between 2000 and 2007
World Index Number: QC/61-11-02
Formerly Listed in County: Brome

Pont de la Frontière (Province Hill)
Region: Cantons de l'Est, Québec
Township: Potton

GPS Position: 45°00'42.0"N 72°22'25.0"W
Directions: From Province Hill, head southwest on Chem. de Province Hill for 2.0 km and turn left onto Chem. du Pont Couvert and the bridge
Crosses: Ruisseau Mud
Carries: Chem. du Pont Couvert
Builder: Not known
Year Built: 1896
Truss Type: Town
Dimensions: 1 Span, 31 meters, 102 feet
Notes: This road originally led to the U.S, border but is now closed. The bridge itself was bypassed in the 1960s. There is a picnic table on the deck,.

World Index Number: QC/61-11-03
Formerly Listed in County: Brome

Pont Drouin

Region: Cantons de l'Est, Québec
Township: Compton

GPS Position: 45°15'50.0"N 71°51'05.0"W
Directions: From Waterville, head east on Rue Compton E for 800 m and continue onto Chem. Compton E. After 2.0 km, turn left onto Chem. Drouin and the bridge is 1.1 km
Crosses: Riviére Coaticook
Carries: Chem. Drouin
Builder: Not known
Year Built: 1886 (R1960)
Truss Type: Multiple kingpost
Dimensions: 1 Span, 30 meters, 98 feet
Notes: In 1960, it was reinforced by the addition of steel beams. The bridge was closed in the 1970s. In 1988 it was due to be demolished but was saved by local volunteers. The abutments were repaired in 2002.
World Index Number: QC/61-18-01
Formerly Listed in County: Compton

Pont d'Eustis
Region: Cantons de l'Est, Québec
Township: Compton

GPS Position: 45°18'11.0"N 71°54'48.0"W
Directions: From Eustis, head southeast on Rue Stafford for 800 m and you will see the bridge
Crosses: Riviére Massawippi
Carries: Rue Stafford
Builder: Hamlet Heavy Timberwork
Year Built: 2011
Truss Type: Multiple kingpost
Dimensions: 1 Span, 27 meters, 90 feet

Notes: The original bridge at this site was built in 1908. It was repaired in 1998 but began to sag in a few years. It was replaced in 2011

World Index Number: QC/61-18-02#2
Formerly Listed in County: Compton

Pont John-Cook
Region: Cantons de l'Est, Québec
Township: Eaton

GPS Position: 45°25'19.0"N 71°37'57.0"W
Directions: From Cookshire-Eaton, head north on Rue Craig N/QC-253 N of Highway 103 for 1.0 km and see the bridge
Crosses: Riviére Eaton
Carries: Rue Craig N/QC-253 N
Builder: Not known
Year Built: 1868 (R2008) (R2015)
Truss Type: Town variation
Dimensions: 1 Span, 41 meters, 133 feet

Notes: The bridge is named for Captain John Cook (1770-1819), one of the first settlers in the area. The structure was closed in the 1970s and both portals were blocked in 2019.

World Index Number: QC/61-18-04
Formerly Listed in County: Compton

Pont McDermott
Region: Cantons de l'Est, Québec
Township: Eaton

GPS Position: 45°23'34.0"N 71°33'22.0"W
Directions: From Lake's Mill, head southeast on Chem.
Flanders for 2.2 km and turn left onto Chem. McDermott and
the bridge is 1.3 km
Crosses: Rivière Eaton, North Branch
Carries: Chem. McDermott
Builder: Not known
Year Built: 1886 (R1989)
Truss Type: Multiple kingpost
Dimensions: 1 Span, 34 meters, 112 feet
Notes: In 1989 the deck and the bridge panel were rebuilt.
The structure was closed in 2003, but reopened in 2008 after
repairs were made

World Index Number: QC/61-18-06
Formerly Listed in County: Compton

Pont McVetty-McKenzie
Region: Cantons de l'Est, Québec
Township: Lingwick

GPS Position: 45°37'10.0"N 71°23'42.0"W
Directions: From Gould, head north on QC-257 N and the bridge is 3.3 km
Crosses: Riviére au Saumon
Carries: QC-257 N
Builder: J. & J.A. McKenzie and William McVetty
Year Built: 1893 (R1950) (R2003)
Truss Type: Town
Dimensions: 2 Spans, 63 meters, 206 feet
Notes: In 1950, the shingle roof was blown off and was replaced by a corrugated steel roof. The bridge was closed in 1979. in 1991, the name was changed from Fisher Hill Bridge to the McVetty-Mcvetty Bridge in honour of its builders. The site has picnic tables, parking and toilets.
World Index Number: QC/61-18-08
Formerly Listed in County: Compton

Pont Guthrie (Pigeon Hill)
Region: Cantons de l'Est, Québec
Township: Seigneurie Saint-Amand

GPS Position: 45°03'56.0"N 72°57'29.0"W
Directions: From Campbell Corners, head north on Chem. Dalpé for 2.0 km and turn right onto Chem. Edoin where the bridge is 600 m
Crosses: Ruisseau Groat
Carries: Chem. Edoin
Builder: Not known
Year Built: CA. 1888 (R1993)
Truss Type: Town
Dimensions: 1 Span, 15 meters, 49 feet
Notes: At 49 feet, this is the shortest public covered bridge in Quebec. The structure was repaired in 1993. The bridge is named for a family that lived nearby

World Index Number: QC/61-45-01
Formerly Listed in County: Missisquoi

Pont de Freeport (Cowansville)
Region: Cantons de l'Est, Québec
Township: Dunham

GPS Position: 45°13'06.0"N 72°46'02.0"W
Directions: From Cowansville, head northwest on Rue Albert toward for 2.4 km and turn left onto Rue Bell where you find the bridge in 350 m
Crosses: Southeast Yamaska River
Carries: Rue Bel
Builder: Not known
Year Built: 1870 (R2017) (R2020)
Truss Type: Town
Dimensions: 1 Span, 28 meters, 91 feet
Notes: The Bridge was heavily damaged by a truck in 2017 and again in 2020. It was named in honour of Freeman Eldridge, a builder of the area.

World Index Number: QC/61-45-02
Formerly Listed in County: Missisquoi

Pont des Rivières (Pike)
Region: Cantons de l'Est, Québec
Township: Stanbridge

GPS Position: 45°09'28.0"N 73°03'04.0"W
Directions: From Malmaison, head northeast on Chem. des Rivières for 1.5 km and turn right onto Chem. Saint-Charles and the bridge
Crosses: Riviére aux Brochets
Carries: Chem. Saint-Charles
Builder: Joseph Reid and son
Year Built: 1884 (R1998)
Truss Type: Howe
Dimensions: 1 Span, 41 meters, 136 feet
Notes: The bridge is named after the brothers François-Guillaume and Henri Desrivières who built a sawmill and flour mill nearby. In 1998, the bridge was restored including the abutments, the roof and the flooring
World Index Number: QC/61-45-03
Formerly Listed in County: Missisquoi

Pont Cousineau (Bombardier)
Region: Cantons de l'Est, Québec
Township: Ely

GPS Position: 45°29'54.0"N 72°18'50.0"W
Directions: From Valcourt, head north on Rue St Joseph for 500 m and turn right onto Rue du Moulin and the bridge
Crosses: Ruisseau Brandy
Carries: Rue du Moulin
Builder: Not known
Year Built: 1888
Truss Type: Town (R1960) (R1995)
Dimensions: 1 Span, 14 meters, 46 feet
Notes: The bridge is named for the Cousineau family who have owned the bridge since it was built. In 1960, reinforcement beams were added under the bridge. It was repainted in 1995. It is painted white inside and out.

World Index Number: QC/61-66-02
Formerly Listed in County: Shefford

Pont de Milby
Region: Cantons de l'Est, Québec
Township: Ascot

GPS Position: 45°18'54.0"N 71°49'23.0"W
Directions: From Milby, head north on QC-147 N for 200 m and turn right onto Chem. du Pont Couvert to find the bridge
Crosses: Riviére Moe
Carries: Chem. du Pont Couvert
Builder: Robert and John Hood
Year Built: 1873 (R1997) (R2007)
Truss Type: Town
Dimensions: 1 Span, 23 meters, 75 feet
Notes: In 1997, the roof and side panels were renewed. The bridge was closed to traffic in 2003 when it was found unsafe. In 2007, the bridge received a major restoration. The bridge was reopened seasonally in 2009. In 2023, it was changed to one-way traffic.
World Index Number: QC/61-67-03
Formerly Listed in County: Sherbrooke

Pont Rue Saint-Marc
Region: Cantons de l'Est, Québec
Township: Barnston

GPS Position: 45°08'43.8"N 71°47'54.2"W
Directions: From the town of Coaticook-Nord, head southeast on Rue Saint-Marc from Highway 147 and the bridge is 750 m
Crosses: Coaticook
Carries: Rue Saint-Marc
Builder: Technika
Year Built: 1998
Truss Type: Multiple kingpost
Dimensions: 1 Span, 18 meters, 61 feet
Notes: The original covered bridge at this site was built in 1887 and removed in 1979. The present bridge was built by Technika in 1998. The bridge is located at Parc de la Gorge in Coaticook.

World Index Number: QC/61-69-02#2
Formerly Listed in County: Stanstead

Pont Narrows
Region: Cantons de l'Est, Québec
Township: Stanstead

GPS Position: 45°05'32.0"N 72°12'03.0"W
Directions: From Applegrove, head northwest on Chem. Narrows for 1km and turn left onto Chem. d'Arrow Head. After 230 m make a left onto Chem. Ridgewood and the bridge
Crosses: Fitch Bay Narrows
Carries: Chem. Ridgewood
Builder: Charles and Alexander McPherson
Year Built: 1881
Truss Type: Town
Dimensions: 1 Span, 28 meters, 92 feet
Notes: The bridge was closed to traffic in 1977. Painted fences and flower boxes were added in 2015. The interior of the bridge was repainted in white in 2019 which hid some of the graffiti it has suffered.
World Index Number: QC/61-69-03
Formerly Listed in County: Stanstead

Pont Perreault
Region: Centre-du-Quebec, Québec
Township: Warwick

GPS Position: 46°10'57.5"N 70°43'00.1"W
Directions: From Notre-Dame-des-Pins, head west on 30e Rue from Highway 173 and the bridge is 650 m
Crosses: Riviére des Pins
Carries: 30e Rue
Builder: Not known
Year Built: 1929 (R2011)
Truss Type: Town variation
Dimensions: 1 Span, 29 meters, 97 feet

Notes: This bridge was closed to traffic in 1957. The structure was restored in 2011 by Construction Giron. The bridge honours Minister Joseph-Édouard-Perrault.

World Index Number: QC/61-04-06
Formerly Listed in County: Arthabaska

Pont Descormiers
Region: Centre-du-Quebec, Québec
Township: Tingwick

GPS Position: 45°53'51"N71°46'38"W
Directions: From Le Pont-Rouge, head southwest on Rang 10e et 11e/Rang Leclerc for 850 m and turn left on unnamed rd where the bridge is 700 m
Crosses: Ruisseau Laflamme
Carries: Unnamed road
Builder: Not known
Year Built: 1904 (R2011) (R2020)
Truss Type: Multiple Kingpost
Dimensions: 1 Span, 9 meters, 29 feet
Notes: The bridge is on private property. It received its name from former owners of the farm. The structure was restored in 2011 after it began to sink. New entrance ramps were added in 2020
World Index Number: QC/61-04-07
Formerly Listed in County: Arthabaska

Pont Davitt (Monaghan)
Region: Centre-du-Quebec, Québec
Township: Drummondville

GPS Position: 45°53'37.2"N 72°29'18.6"W
Directions: 1370 Rue Montplaisir, Drummondville
Crosses: small creek
Carries: Rue Montplaisir
Builder: Not known
Year Built: 1878 (M1983)
Truss Type: Howe
Dimensions: 1 Span, 16 meters, 53 feet
Notes: This bridge was built in 1878 and located at Stanbridge East crossing the Rivière aux Brochets. It was disassembled in 1983 and reconstructed in Drummondville at the Village Québécois d'Antan. Each piece was numbered so it could be reconstructed . There is an admission charge.

World Index Number: QC/61-21-01
Formerly Listed in County: Drummond

Pont Paul-Émile-Giguère
Region: **Centre-du-Quebec, Québec**
Township: **Durham**

GPS Position: 45°41'26.8"N 72°16'11.6"W
Directions: From Richmond, follow QC-116 O to 9e Rang in Sainte-Christine for 11.6 km and continue on Rte Lisgar and Chem. Lisgar for 5.8 km where you will see the bridge
Crosses: Ulverton River
Carries: Chem. Lisgar
Builder: Not known
Year Built: 1994
Truss Type: Town
Dimensions: 1 Span, 22 meters, 72 feet
Notes: The original bridge was built in 1885 near the Ulverton Woolen Mill. It was demolished in the 1950s. The second bridge, built in 1992, burned down in 1993. The present bridge was built in 1994.
World Index Number: QC/61-21-05#3
Formerly Listed in County: Drummond

Pont Lambert
Region: Centre-du-Quebec, Québec
Township: Halifax

GPS Position: 46°07'41.0"N 71°45'55.0"W
Directions: From La Rochelle, head southeast on 2e Rang for 1.4 km and turn right onto Rte Lambert to see the bridge
Crosses: Riviére Bulstrode
Carries: Rte Lambert
Builder: Not known
Year Built: 1948 (M1925) (R2018) (R2020) (R2023)
Truss Type: Town variation
Dimensions: 1 Span, 27 meters, 89 feet

Notes: The bridge was originally called the Poirier bridge after a local family. In 1925, it was moved to its current location. In 2023 it was repainted white.

World Index Number: QC/61-44-08
Formerly Listed in County: Mégantic

Pont des Raymond
Region: Centre-du-Quebec, Québec
Township: Aston

GPS Position: 46°15'36.0"N 72°24'08.0"W
Directions: From Saint-Célestin-Station, head north on Rang Saint-Michel for 3.8 km and turn left onto Rte de la Seine and the bridge is 1.8 km
Crosses: Rivière Saint-Wenceslas (Blanche)
Carries: Rte de la Seine
Builder: Not known
Year Built: 1928
Truss Type: Town variation
Dimensions: 1 Span, 30 meters, 97 feet
Notes: Arson attacks were made on the structure twice in 2000. It is closed in the winter although still easy to see. It has a load capacity of 12 tonnes

World Index Number: QC/61-51-01
Formerly Listed in County: Nicolet

Pont-Etienne Poirier (Sainte-Cèlestine)
Region: Centre-du-Quebec, Québec
Township: Aston

GPS Position: 46°11'50.0"N 72°23'24.0"W
Directions: From Saint-Célestin, head northeast on QC-226 E for 1.7 km and continue onto Anc. Rte 161. In 3.9 km turn right onto Rang Pellerin and the bridge is 1.0 km
Crosses: Rivière Saint-Wenceslas (Blanche)
Carries: Rang Pellerin
Builder: Not known
Year Built: 1905
Truss Type: Town variation
Dimensions: 1 Span, 25 meters, 81 feet
Notes: The road is closed in the winter but the bridge is easy to visit. Height restrictors were installed in 1991. The bridge is named for a local pioneer from the area

World Index Number: QC/61-51-03
Formerly Listed in County: Nicolet

Pont de Saint-Placide-de-Charlevoix
Region: Charlevoix, Québec
Township: Seigneurie Beaupré

GPS Position: 47°24'28.0"N 70°37'03.0"W
Directions: From Saint-Placide-de-Charlevoix, head southwest on Rang St Placide S for 60 m and turn left onto Chem. du Pont Couvert and the bridge is 700 m
Crosses: Rivière Bras du Nord-Ouest
Carries: Chem. du Pont Couvert
Builder: Joseph Normandeau
Year Built: 1926 (R1995) (R2023)
Truss Type: Town variation
Dimensions: 1 Span, 34 meters, 113 feet
Notes: The road was previously closed in winter but is now open after improvements. The load capacity was changed to 5 tonnes from 12 in 2012. The roof was replaced in 2023 after damage by snow load.
World Index Number: QC/61-14-03
Formerly Listed in County: Charlevoix

Pont Perrault
Region: Chaudière-Appalaches, Québec
Township: Seigneurie Rigaud/Vaudreuil

GPS Position: 45°57'23.0"N 72°00'24.0"W
Directions: From Warwick, head northwest on Rte St Albert for 1.0 km and the bridge
Crosses: Rivière Chaudière
Carries: Rte St Albert
Builder: Not known
Year Built: 1928 (R2022)
Truss Type: Town variation
Dimensions: 4 Span, 150 meters, 495 feet
Notes: At 495 feet, the bridge is the second longest covered bridge in Quebec. The bridge was closed to vehicle traffic in 1969. After the 2022 restoration, the bridge was opened to pedestrian and cycle traffic

World Index Number: QC/61-06-01
Formerly Listed in County: Beauce

Pont Bolduc
Region: Chaudière-Appalaches, Québec
Township: Tring

GPS Position: 46°07'43.0"N 70°59'15.0"W
Directions: From Sainte-Clotilde-de-Beauce, head northeast on Rte du Moulin for 2.7 km and turn right onto 7e Rang/Rang 7e N where the bridge is 2.0 km
Crosses: Rivière Fortin-Dupuis
Carries: 7e Rang/Rang 7e N
Builder: Lucien Bolduc
Year Built: 1937 (M1942)
Truss Type: Town variation
Dimensions: 1Span, 21 meters, 73 feet
Notes: In 2012 it was decided to move the bridge 13 meters to build a modern bridge in its place. The structure was moved from its abutments to a field and in 2014 it was replaced on the new ones. There is parking and picnic tables provided.
World Index Number: QC/61-06-02
Formerly Listed in County: Beauce

Pont Napoléon-Grondin
Region: Chaudière-Appalaches, Québec
Township: Schenley

GPS Position: 46°03'31.7"N 70°54'29.2"W
Directions: From Saint-Éphrem-de-Beauce, head northeast on QC-271 S for 4.3 km ,and you will find the bridge
Crosses: small brook
Carries: QC-271 S
Builder: Not known
Year Built: 1933 (M1992) (R1993)
Truss Type: Town variation
Dimensions: 1 Span, 20 meters, 65 feet

Notes: The bridge was damaged by a storm in 1992 and a few days later. Pierre Mathieu moved the structure to private property and then reconstructed a shorter version.

World Index Number: QC/61-06-06
Formerly Listed in County: Beauce

Pont du Sault
Region: Chaudière-Appalaches, Québec
Township: Casgrain

GPS Position: 46°55'08.0"N 69°53'46.0"W
Directions: From Saint-Pamphile, head southwest on QC-204 O for 9.4 km and turn right onto Rte du Sault. After 3.3 km turn right onto 4e Rang E and the bridge
Crosses: Grande Rivière Noir
Carries: 4e Rang E
Builder: Not known
Year Built: 1943 (R1990) (R1998)
Truss Type: Town variation
Dimensions: 1 Span, 39 meters, 129 feet
Notes: Major repairs were made in 1990. This included painting the panelling grey with red mouldings. The panelling had formerly been yellow. The approaches were repaired in 1998.
World Index Number: QC/61-39-01
Formerly Listed in County: L'Islet

Pont Saint-André
Region: Chaudière-Appalaches, Québec
Township: Seigneurie Saint-Gilles

GPS Position: 46°21'34.0"N 71°19'14.0"W
Directions: From Wilson, head west on Rte de Ste Agathe/QC-271 N for 3.5 km and turn right onto Rang St Michel. After 2.5 km continue onto Rang St André/Rte St André and the bridge is 1.2 km
Crosses: Rivière Filkars
Carries: Rang St André/Rte St André
Builder: Not known
Year Built: 1927 (R2002) (R2013)
Truss Type: Town variation
Dimensions: 1 Span, 25 meters, 81 feet
Notes: The bridge was bypassed in 1992 and a picnic area was developed at the site. It was formerly blue-gray but was painted red in 2002
World Index Number: QC/61-40-03
Formerly Listed in County: Lotbinière

Pont Caron
Region: Chaudière-Appalaches, Québec
Township: Seigneurie Lotbinière

GPS Position: 46°25'19.0"N 71°42'20.0"W
Directions: From Val-Alain, head southeast on Rue de la Station for 1.6 km and continue onto 1er Rang where the bridge is 3.0 km
Crosses: Grande Rivière du Chêne
Carries: 1er Rang
Builder: Romain Caron
Year Built: 1933 or 1942
Truss Type: Town variation
Dimensions: 1 Span, 25 meters, 81 feet
Notes: The bridge is named for the builder, Romain Caron. The bridge was closed to vehicular traffic in 1979. Shortly after the bridge was closed, the roof collapsed due to a high snow load. A park was added in 2013
World Index Number: QC/61-40-04
Formerly Listed in County: Lotbinière

Pont Rouge (Sainte-Agathe)
Region: Chaudière-Appalaches, Québec
Township: Nelson

GPS Position: 46°19'50.0"N 71°24'53.0"W
Directions: From Sainte-Agathe, head south on Chem. Gosford/Rue Gosford O for 4.6 km and turn left onto Chem. Gosford where the bridge is 2.6 km
Crosses: Rivière Palmer
Carries: Chem. Gosford
Builder: Not known
Year Built: 1928 (R2007) (2013)
Truss Type: Town variation
Dimensions: 1 Span, 39 meters, 129 feet
Notes: A park has been built at the site which has become very popular. The bridge was restored in 2007. In 2013, height restrictors were added.

World Index Number: QC/61-44-01
Formerly Listed in County: Mégantic

Pont des Défricheurs
Region: Chaudière-Appalaches, Québec
Township: Talon

GPS Position: 46°45'15.0"N 70°03'33.0"W
Directions: From Sainte-Lucie-de-Beauregard, head northwest on Rte des Chutes for 3.4 km to find the bridge
Crosses: Rivière Noire Nord-Ouest
Carries: Rte des Chutes
Builder: Not known
Year Built: 1936 (R1970) (R2016)
Truss Type: Town variation
Dimensions: 1 Span, 30 meters, 97 feet
Notes: The bridge was painted orange in the 1970s. The structure was badly damaged in August 2016 and closed to traffic for about 4 months. It was restored and reopened in late 2016. It is named after early settlers

World Index Number: QC/61-47-02
Formerly Listed in County: Montmagny

Pont des Pionniers
Region: Eeyou Istchee Baie-James, Québec
Township: Rousseau

GPS Position: 49°07'35.8"N 79°15'16.6"W
Directions: From Val-Paradis, head east on Chem. des 10e-et-1er-Rangs/QC-393 S for 2.8 km and take a slight right onto QC-393 S, After 3.2 km turn right onto Chem. des 8e et 9e Rangs and the bridge is 1.1 km
Crosses: Ruisseau Leslie
Carries: Chem. des 8e et 9e Rangs
Builder: Ministry of Colonization
Year Built: 1943 (R1985) (R1992)
Truss Type: Town variation
Dimensions: 1 Span, 25 meters, 81 feet
Notes: The bridge is named for the settlers to the area. A restoration was performed in 1985 and the bridge was painted red from its former gray. The roof was replaced in 1992.
World Index Number: QC/61-02-32
Formerly Listed in County: Abitibi-Ouest

Pont des Souvenirs
Region: Eeyou Istchee Baie-James, Québec
Township: Rousseau

GPS Position: 49°02'18.9"N 79°10'50.9"W
Directions: From Beaucanton, head east on Chem. des 2 et 3 Rangs for 4.2 km where you will see the bridge
Crosses: Rivière Turgeon
Carries: Chem. des 2 et 3 Rangs
Builder: Ministry of Colonization
Year Built: 1954
Truss Type: Town variation
Dimensions: 2 Spans, 44 meters, 145 feet

Notes: In 1995, the maximum load was reduced from 12 tonnes to 5 tonnes. The name honours the first settlers in the area. In 2010 the bridge was closed to vehicular traffic.

World Index Number: QC/61-02-33
Formerly Listed in County: Abitibi-Ouest

Pont Maurice-Duplessis
Region: Eeyou Istchee Baie-James, Québec
Township: Rousseau

GPS Position: 49°04'04.0"N 79°10'30.0"W
Directions: From Beasucanton, head north on QC-393 N for 3.2 km and turn right onto Chem. des 4 et 5 Rangs. After 4.7 km you will find the bridge
Crosses: Rivière Turgeon
Carries: Chem. des 4 et 5 Rangs
Builder: Ministry of Colonization
Year Built: 1948 (R1984)
Truss Type: Town variation
Dimensions: 1 Span, 30 meters, 97 feet
Notes: A major restoration was performed in 1984 which included modifying the side windows. It was also repainted gray at that time.

World Index Number: QC/61-02-34
Formerly Listed in County: Abitibi-Ouest

Pont Taschereau
Region: Eeyou Istchee Baie-James, Québec
Township: Rousseau

GPS Position: 49°07'35.0"N 79°12'03.0"W
Directions: From Villebois, head north on Rte des Conquérants for 2.8 km and turn left onto Chem. des 8e et 9e Rangs. After 3.9 km you will find the bridge
Crosses: Rivière Turgeon
Carries: Chem. des 8e et 9e Rangs
Builder: Ministry of Colonization
Year Built: 1939
Truss Type: Town variation
Dimensions: 1 Span, 44 meters, 145 feet
Notes: The bridge was named in honour of Louis-Alexandre Taschereau, former Premier of Quebec. It has been closed to traffic since August 2009. The structure was formerly painted red but looks unpainted due to wear.
World Index Number: QC/61-02-39
Formerly Listed in County: Abitibi-Ouest

Pont de Saint-Edgar
Region: Gaspésie, Québec
Township: New Richmond

GPS Position: 48°14'15.0"N 65°43'32.0"W
Directions: From Chaleurs, head northeast on Chem. de Saint-Edgar for 11.5 km and turn left onto Rue du Pont where you will see the bridge
Crosses: Petit Rivière Cascapédia
Carries: Rue du Pont
Builder: Not known
Year Built: 1938 (R2014)
Truss Type: Town variation
Dimensions: 2 Spans, 89 meters, 293 feet
Notes: The bridge was painted red in 1980, having previously been gray. The bridge was bypassed and closed to highway traffic in 2008. It was restored in 2014 by Construction LFG

World Index Number: QC/61-10-05
Formerly Listed in County: Bonaventure

Pont Galipeault
Region: Gaspésie, Québec
Township: Seigneurie de la Grande-Vallée

GPS Position: 49°13'21.0"N 65°07'33.0"W
Directions: From Grande-Vallée, head NW on Rue St François Xavier E for 210 m and turn right onto Rue de la Fabrique. After 19 m make a slight right onto Rue du Vieux Pont and the bridge is 400 m
Crosses: Rivière de la Grande-Vallèe
Carries: Rue du Vieux Pont
Builder: Not known
Year Built: 1923 (R1985) (R2016)
Truss Type: Town variation
Dimensions: 1 Span, 44 meters, 145 feet
Notes: Metal support added around 1985 to strengthen the structure. Major restoration work carried out in 2016. It still carries vehicle traffic.
World Index Number: QC/61-23-01
Formerly Listed in County: Gaspé-Nord

Pont Jean-Chassé (St. Luc)
Region: Gaspésie, Québec
Township: Tessier

GPS Position: 48°43'12.0"N 67°24'50.0"W
Directions: From Ruisseau-Gagnon, head southwest on Rte de la Montagne and the bridge is found in 110 m
Crosses: Rivière Matane
Carries: Rte de la Montagne
Builder: Not known
Year Built: 1945 (R2000)
Truss Type: Town variation
Dimensions: 1 Span, 44 meters, 145 feet
Notes: This bridge is named for Jean Chassé, the original owner of the land at the site. The bridge was restored in 2000 by company C. J. Picard. At this time a steel bridge was built and the old framework was attached.

World Index Number: QC/61-42-01
Formerly Listed in County: Matane

Pont Bélanger (Les Boules)
Region: Gaspésie, Québec
Township: MacNider

GPS Position: 48°38'08.0"N 67°54'20.0"W
Directions: From MacNider, head SW on Av. Principale for 850 m and turn right onto Rue de l'Église. Continue onto 7e Rang O for 7.0 km and turn right onto Rte Macnider where the site is 2.6 km
Crosses: Rivière Tartigou
Carries: Rte Macnider
Builder: Not known
Year Built: 1925 (R1993) (R2002)
Truss Type: Town variation
Dimensions: 1 Span, 27 meters, 88 feet
Notes: The bridge was damaged in 1992 and repaired by 1993. Repair work in 2002 include replacement of panelling. It was named for a pioneer family.
World Index Number: QC/61-42-04
Formerly Listed in County: Matane

Pont Pierre-Carrier
Region: Gaspésie, Québec
Township: Matane

GPS Position: 48°46'20.0"N 67°41'05.0"W
Directions: From Saint-Ulric, head SW on Rte James for 1.9 km and turn left onto Chem. du Pont Couvert where the bridge is 500 m
Crosses: Blanche
Carries: Chem. du Pont Couvert
Builder: Not known
Year Built: 1918 (R2010) (R2016)
Truss Type: Town variation
Dimensions: 1 Span, 25 meters, 81 feet
Notes: The bridge is named for Pierre Carrier, a pioneer of the area. The site was restored in 2010. The portals were damaged in 2016 and repaired the same year.

World Index Number: QC/61-42-05
Formerly Listed in County: Matane

Pont François-Gagnon (Saint-René-de-Matane)
Region: Gaspésie, Québec
Township: Tessier

GPS Position: 48°42'24.0"N 67°23'22.0"W
Directions: In Saint-René-de-Matane, head southwest from QC-195 on Rue Degas for a short distance to see the bridge
Crosses: Rivière Matane
Carries: Rue Degas
Builder: Not known
Year Built: 1942 (R1995) (R2018)
Truss Type: Town variation
Dimensions: 1 Span, 52 meters, 170 feet

Notes: In 1995, a steel substructure was added, making the town truss nonfunctional. It was painted red from its former gray, in 1996. It remains open to traffic.

World Index Number: QC/61-42-06
Formerly Listed in County: Matane

Pont Heppell
Region: Gaspésie, Québec
Township: Matalik-Casapscull

GPS Position: 48°18'43.0"N 67°14'29.0"W
Directions: From the town of Heppell, head west on Rte Heppell from Rte 132 E for a short distance to see the bridge.
Crosses: Rivière Matapédia
Carries: Rte Heppell
Builder: Not known
Year Built: 1909 (R1991) (R2018)
Truss Type: Town variation
Dimensions: 1 Span, 39 meters, 129 feet

Notes: The bridge was badly damaged by a 1991 flood and was repaired the same year. It was hard hit by water again in 2017. It was repaired by the next year.

World Index Number: QC/61-43-02
Formerly Listed in County: Matapédia

Pont de Routhierville
Region: Gaspésie, Québec
Township: Milnikek-Assemetquagan

GPS Position: 48°10'56.0"N 67°08'57.0"W
Directions: From Milnikek, head northeast on Chem. du 2 Rang Matalik for 5.7 km and turn right onto Chem. du Rang A where the bridge is 1.9 km
Crosses: Rivière Matapédia
Carries: Chem. du Rang A
Builder: Not known
Year Built: 1931 (R1994) (R2012) (R2021)
Truss Type: Town variation
Dimensions: 2 Spans, 79 meters, 259 feet
Notes: The repairs in 1994 were needed after heavy flood damage. A restoration was done between 2010 and 2012. It was closed for repairs in 2021 and reopened the same year.

World Index Number: QC/61-43-04
Formerly Listed in County: Matapédia

Pont de l'Anse-Saint-Jean (Amqui)
Region: Gaspésie, Québec
Township: Seigneurie du lac Matapédia

GPS Position: 48°29'31.0"N 67°26'54.0"W
Directions: From Amqui, head west on QC-132 E for 3.3 km and turn right onto Chem. du Pont Couvert where you find the bridge
Crosses: Rivière Matapédia
Carries: Chem. du Pont Couvert
Builder: Not known
Year Built: 1931 (R1970s)
Truss Type: Town variation
Dimensions: 1+ Span, 44 meters, 145 feet
Notes: A center pier was added in the 1950s. It was restored in the 1970s. In 1990 it was decided to demolish the structure but it was saved after local protests.

World Index Number: QC/61-43-05
Formerly Listed in County: Matapédia

Pont Beauséjour
Region: Gaspésie, Québec
Township: Seigneurie du lac Matapédia

GPS Position: 48°27'58.0"N 67°26'00.0"W
Directions: In Amqui, head northeast on Rue du Pont from 132 for 250 m and turn left onto Rue Desbiens. After 200 m turn left onto Rue Ste Ursule where you see the bridge
Crosses: Rivière Matapédia
Carries: Rue Ste Ursule
Builder: Not known
Year Built: 1932 (M2005)
Truss Type: Town variation
Dimensions: 1 Span, 37 meters, 122 feet
Notes: The bridge was removed from its original location in Rimouski County in 2003 and was reconstructed in a public park in Amqui in 2005

World Index Number: QC/61-43-25
Formerly Listed in County: Matapédia

Pont Grandchamp
Region: Lanaudière, Québec
Township: Seigneurie Berthier

GPS Position: 46°05'35.4"N 73°12'41.0"W
Directions: From Berthierville, head northwest on Bd Gilles Villeneuve/QC-158 O for 2.3 km
Crosses: Rivière Berthier
Carries: Bd Gilles Villeneuve/QC-158 O
Builder: Not known
Year Built: c.1918 (R1996) (R1998)
Truss Type: Town variation
Dimensions: 1 Span, 34 meters, 113 feet

Notes: The bridge was closed to traffic in 1977. Steel beams were installed in 1966 and the bridge was reopened. In 1998 the roof was repaired and the bridge was repainted

World Index Number: QC/61-09-02
Formerly Listed in County: Berthier

Grand pont de Ferme Rouge
Region: Laurentides, Québec
Township: Bouthillier - Kiamika

GPS Position: 46°25'35.0"N 75°25'44.5"W
Directions: From Kiamika, head northwest on Chem. de Frm Rouge for 3.7 km and turn right onto Chem. de Frm Rouge. In 600 m turn left onto Chem. de Kiamika and the bridge
Crosses: Rivière du Lièvre
Carries: Chem. de Kiamika
Builder: Not known
Year Built: 1903
Truss Type: Town variation
Dimensions: 2 Spans, 77 meters, 251 feet
Notes: This is the longer of a pair of bridges at this site. It was closed for a few days in spring 2018 and spring 2019 due to flooding.

World Index Number: QC/61-33-02
Formerly Listed in County: Labelle

Petit pont de Ferme Rouge
Region: Laurentides, Québec
Township: Bouthillier - Kiamika

GPS Position: 46°25'35.1"N 75°25'40.0"W
Directions: From Kiamika, head northwest on Chem. de Frm Rouge for 3.7 km and turn right onto Chem. de Frm Rouge. In 600 m turn left onto Chem. de Kiamika and the bridge
Crosses: Rivière du Lièvre
Carries: Chem. de Kiamika
Builder: Not known
Year Built: 1903
Truss Type: Town variation
Dimensions: 2 Span, 49 meters, 162 feet
Notes: This is the shorter of a pair of bridges at this site. It was closed for a few days in spring 2018 and spring 2019 due to flooding.

World Index Number: QC/61-33-03
Formerly Listed in County: Labelle

Pont Armand Lachaîne
Region: Laurentides, Québec
Township: Rochon-Moreau

GPS Position: 46°38'36.0"N 75°16'08.0"W
Directions: From Lac-Saint-Paul, head south on QC-311 S for
12.2 km and turn right onto Chem. du Progrès for 280 m. Turn
left onto Chem. du Vieux Pont and the bridge
Crosses: Rivière Kiamika
Carries: Chem. du Vieux Pont
Builder: Not known
Year Built: 1904 (R2024)
Truss Type: Town variation
Dimensions: 1 Span, 35 meters, 113 feet
Notes: The structure was closed to all vehicle traffic after an
accident occurred in May 2024 but was reopened shortly. The
bridge was painted red in 2007, from the former white

World Index Number: QC/61-33-05
Formerly Listed in County: Labelle

Pont Macaza
Region: Laurentides, Québec
Township: Marchand

GPS Position: 46°21'24.0"N 74°46'46.0"W
Directions: From Macaza, head east on Chem. des Cascades for 400 m and turn left onto Chem. du Pont Couvert to find the bridge
Crosses: Rivière Macaza
Carries: Chem. du Pont Couvert
Builder: Not known
Year Built: 1904 (R1993) (R2016)
Truss Type: Town variation
Dimensions: 1+ Span, 39 meters, 129 feet
Notes: The bridge was raised and repainted in 1993. There is a picnic table and parking at the site. It underwent a restoration in 2016.

World Index Number: QC/61-33-10
Formerly Listed in County: Labelle

Pont Prud'homme
Region: Laurentides, Québec
Township: de Salaberry

GPS Position: 46°04'22.0"N 74°37'30.0"W
Directions: From Crystal Falls, head northwest on QC-327 N for 2.7 km and turn left onto Chem. du Pont Prud'homme where the bridge is a short distance
Crosses: du Diable
Carries: Chem. du Pont Prud'homme
Builder: Not known
Year Built: 1918 (R1997)
Truss Type: Town variation
Dimensions: 1 Span, 44 meters, 145 feet
Notes: The bridge was restored in 1997 and painted red at that time. It was closed to all traffic in 2019. The site has parking and picnic tables.

World Index Number: QC/61-72-01
Formerly Listed in County: Terrebonne

Pont Louis-Gravel
Region: Manicougan, Québec
Township: Albert

GPS Position: 48°16'04.0"N 69°54'31.0"W
Directions: From Rivière Sainte-Marguerite, head northwest on QC-172 O for 3.4 km and turn left onto Chem. du Vieux-Pont. After 450 m turn left to stay on Chem. du Vieux-Pont and you will see the bridge
Crosses: Rivière Sainte-Marguerite Nord-Est
Carries: Chem. du Vieux-Pont
Builder: Not known
Year Built: 1934 (R1999) (R2012)
Truss Type: Town variation
Dimensions: 1 Span, 39 meters, 129 feet
Notes: The bridge collapsed in 1998 and needed major repairs, completed in 1999. This included adding steel beams. In 2012, repairs were needed due to flood damage
World Index Number: QC/61-62-01
Formerly Listed in County: Saguenay

Pont-Émile Lapointe
Region: Manicougan, Québec
Township: Manicougan

GPS Position: 49°05'41.0"N 68°18'38.0"W
Directions: From Baie-Saint-Ludger, head northeast on Chem. de la Baie Saint-Ludger/Rue de Baie St Ludger for 600 m to find the bridge
Crosses: Rivière Saint-Athanase Ouest
Carries: Rue de Baie St Ludger
Builder: Not known
Year Built: 1945 (R1992)
Truss Type: Town variation
Dimensions: 1 Span, 32 meters, 105 feet
Notes: Built in St. Laudger in 1945, this bridge is named for the owner of the sawmill who provided the wood for construction. A major restoration was completed in 1992

World Index Number: QC/61-62-03
Formerly Listed in County: Saguenay

Pont Bordeleau
Region: Mauricie, Québec
Township: Seigneurie Batiscan

GPS Position: 46°40'24.0"N 72°33'28.0"W
Directions: From Saint-Séverin, head southwest on Rue St Georges for 2.1 km and continue onto Chem. de la Rivière des Envies So/Rang S where the bridge is 2.8 km
Crosses: Rivière des Envies
Carries: Chem. de la Rivière des Envies So/Rang S
Builder: Not known
Year Built: 1932 (R2002) (R2010)
Truss Type: Town variation
Dimensions: 1 Span, 33 meters, 109 feet
Notes: The bridge was closed to traffic in 2001 but reopened after 2002 repairs. It was repaired again in 2010, but closed again in 2017. The bridge is now red with white trim previous to being white with green trim
World Index Number: QC/61-13-03
Formerly Listed in County: Champlain

Pont Ducharme (Saint-Jean Bosco)
Region: Mauricie, Québec
Township: Bourgeoys

GPS Position: 47°31'11.0"N 72°40'51.0"W
Directions: From La Tuque, head northeast on Rue de la Rivière for 750 m and turn left onto QC-155 N. After 9.9 km turn right onto Rue de l'Église and the bridge
Crosses: Rivière Saint-Athanase Ouest
Carries: Rue de l'Église
Builder: Not known
Year Built: 1946 (R1997) (R2009)
Truss Type: Town variation
Dimensions: 1 Span, 42 meters, 137 feet
Notes: The Bridge is named for Charles Ducharme who was Member of Parliament. It was restored in 1997, when its colour was changed from white to red. It underwent another restoration in 2009
World Index Number: QC/61-62-03
Formerly Listed in County: Laviolette

Pont Thiffault
Region: Mauricie, Québec
Township: Bourgeoys

GPS Position: 47°33'45.0"N 72°38'15.0"W
Directions: From La Bostonnais, head north on Rang Bostonnais/Rang Sud-Est for 1.1 km and turn left onto Rue de l'Église. After 450 m turn right onto QC-155 N and travel 6.1 km. Turn right onto Rang Bostonnais and see the bridge
Crosses: Rivière Bostonnais
Carries: Rang Bostonnais
Builder: Raymond Thiffault
Year Built: 1946 (R2009)
Truss Type: Town variation
Dimensions: 1 Span, 42 meters, 137 feet
Notes: The name of the bridge commemorates its builder, Raymond Thiffault. It was painted in red in 2009 after being pale green for many years
World Index Number: QC/61-37-03
Formerly Listed in County: Laviolette

Pont de Saint-Mathieu
Region: Mauricie, Québec
Township: Saint-Mathieu

GPS Position: 46°36'10.0"N 72°53'02.0"W
Directions: From Saint-Gérard-des-Laurentides, head SW on QC-351 S for 5.5 km and turn right on Chemin St François. In 700 m, turn right on Chemin du Pont-Couvert and the bridge
Crosses: Rivière Shawinigan
Carries: Chemin du Pont-Couvert
Builder: Not known
Year Built: 1936 (R1974) (R1992) (R2009)
Truss Type: Town variation
Dimensions: 1 Span, 25 meters, 81 feet
Notes: The abutments were repaired and the panelling was repainted in 1974. The abutments were again rebuilt in 1992, when the deck was also replaced. An additional renovation was done in 2009.
World Index Number: QC/61-65-01
Formerly Listed in County: Saint-Maurice

Pont Powerscourt
Region: Montérégie, Québec
Township: Elgin-Hinchinbrook

GPS Position: 45°00'25.0"N 74°09'40.0"W
Directions: From Powerscourt, head west on Chem. de la 1e Concession and the bridge is 120 m
Crosses: Rivière Châteauguay
Carries: Chem. de la 1e Concession
Builder: Robert Graham
Year Built: 1933 (R1949) (R1988)
Truss Type: McCallum
Dimensions: 2 Spans, 50 meters, 165 feet
Notes: The author's image above was featured on a Canadian postage stamp in 2019. In 1983 the Ministère des Transports planned to replace the bridge with a concrete one but the local community saved it. It is the only bridge with a McCallum truss

World Index Number: QC/61-27-01
Formerly Listed in County: Huntingdon

Pont Marois
Region: Outaouais, Québec
Township: Northfield

GPS Position: 46°07'07.5"N 75°56'37.1"W
Directions: From Clément, head west on Chem. de Point Comfort for 600 m to find the bridge
Crosses: affluent de la Gatineau
Carries: Chem. de Point Comfort
Builder: Not known
Year Built: 1933
Truss Type: Town variation
Dimensions: 1 Span, 30 meters, 97 fee5

Notes: This bridge closed in 1966 and was purchased by the Marois family who have lived in the area for many years. It is on private property although they seem open to visitors

World Index Number: QC/61-25-02
Formerly Listed in County: Gatineau

Pont Gendrone (Wakefield)
Region: Outaouais, Québec
Township: Wakefield

GPS Position: 45°38'44.6"N 75°55'06.2"W
Directions: From Wakefield, head north on Chem. Riverside for 950 m and turn right onto Ch Edelweiss. After 450 m turn right on Chem. de Wakefield Heights and the bridge is 500 m
Crosses: Rivière Gatineau
Carries: Chem. de Wakefield Heights
Builder: Local volunteers
Year Built: 1998
Truss Type: Town variation
Dimensions: 2 Span, 89 meters, 389 feet
Notes: The first covered bridge was built at this site in 1915 and burned down in 1984. Local volunteers proposed rebuilding it for pedestrians and cyclists and it was completed in 1998
World Index Number: QC/61-25-07#2
Formerly Listed in County: Gatineau

Pont Cousineau
Region: Outaouais, Québec
Township: Wright

GPS Position: 46°03'57.0"N 76°06'27.0"W
Directions: From Wright County, head west on Chem. du Lac Cayamant for 750 m.Turn left onto Chem. Marks. After 1.1 km turn right on Chem. du Ruisseau des Cerises and the bridge
Crosses: Rivière Picanoc
Carries: Chem. du Ruisseau des Cerises
Builder: Cousineau family
Year Built: 1932 (R1983) (R1995) (R2011)
Truss Type: Town variation
Dimensions: 1 Span, 29 meters, 97 feet
Notes: The name of this bridge honours the memory of the family that built it. In 1995 the bridge was painted white from its former gray. It was completely restored in 2011.

World Index Number: QC/61-25-08
Formerly Listed in County: Gatineau

Pont de l' Aigle
Region: Outaouais, Québec
Township: Egan

GPS Position: 46°27'10.0"N 76°02'41.0"W
Directions: From Maniwaki, head SW on Rue l'Heureux 260 m and turn right onto Chem. Montcerf. After 9.1 km, continue straight onto Chem. de l'Aigle and the bridge
Crosses: Rivière Désert
Carries: Chem. de l'Aigle
Builder: Not known
Year Built: 1925 (R1986) (R2021)
Truss Type: Town variation
Dimensions: 1 Span, 39 meters, 129 feet
Notes: The bridge is named for the road its on as well as a nearby waterway. In 1986, repairs included painting the panelling red and the roof green. The bridge was closed for a few days in May 2019 due to a flood.
World Index Number: QC/61-25-11
Formerly Listed in County: Gatineau

Pont Ruisseau-Meech
Region: Outaouais, Québec
Township: Hull

GPS Position: 45°34'57.0"N 75°53'45.0"W
Directions: From Chemin-des-Pins, head west on Chem.
Pine for 190 m and turn right onto Rte 105 N and then left onto
Chem. Pine. After 900 m turn right onto Chem. Cross Loop
and the bridge is 0.4 km
Crosses: Ruisseau-Meech
Carries: Chem. Cross Loop
Builder: Not known
Year Built: 1924 (R1991) (R2010)
Truss Type: Town variation
Dimensions: 1 Span, 19 meters, 65 feet
Notes: A major restoration took place in 2010. The bridge
was not accessible in 2018-2019 after being closed to traffic
following the collapse of a culvert on the road.
World Index Number: QC/61-25-12
Formerly Listed in County: Gatineau

Pont Savoyard (Grand-Remous)
Region: Outaouais, Québec
Township: Lytton/Sicotte

GPS Position: 46°35'30.0"N 75°55'48.0"W
Directions: From Grand-Remous, head south on Rte 105 S for 3.4 km and turn left onto Chem. Pont Rouge where the bridge is 260 m
Crosses: Rivière Gatineau
Carries: Chem. Pont Rouge
Builder: Not known
Year Built: 1925 (R1972)
Truss Type: Town variation
Dimensions: 2+ Spans, 103 meters, 338 feet
Notes: In 1972, a flood damaged the bridge but was quickly repaired. In 1998, the municipality created a rest area at the site with picnic tables and parking. The structure was restored in the summer of 2011
World Index Number: QC/61-25-15
Formerly Listed in County: Gatineau

Pont Brabant-Philippe
Region: Outaouais, Québec
Township: Gatineau

GPS Position: 45°29'54.0"N 75°35'39.0"W
Directions: From Gatineau, head north on QC-366 O for 700 m and turn right onto Rue Sainte-Rose. After 900 m turn left onto Rue Robert Corbett,then right to the bridge
Crosses: Rivière Blanche
Carries: Rue Leclerc
Builder: Construction FGK
Year Built: 2020
Truss Type: Town variation
Dimensions: 1 Span, 31 meters, 108 feet
Notes: This is the third bridge at this location. The first one was lost to arson in 2011. The second was completed in 2015 but burned again in 2016. The current bridge was built by Construction FGK and opened in 2020.
World Index Number: QC/61-25-34#3
Formerly Listed in County: Gatineau

Pont Roland-Houét
Region: Outaouais, Québec
Township: Gatineau

GPS Position: 45°29'59.5"N 75°36'16.3"W
Directions: From Gatineau, head north on Bd Lorrain/QC-366 O for 210 m and turn right onto Rue Vincent-Legris where the bridge is a short walk
Crosses: Rivière Blanche
Carries: N/A
Builder: Not known
Year Built: 2009
Truss Type: Town variation
Dimensions: 1 Span, 12 meters, 40 feet
Notes: This bridge was built on the White River trail for pedestrians and cyclists. It is the second covered bridge on the trail with plans for two more.

World Index Number: QC/61-25-35
Formerly Listed in County: Gatineau

Pont des Bénévoles
Region: Outaouais, Québec
Township: Gatineau

GPS Position: 45°30'11.2"N 75°36'02.0"W
Directions: In Gatineau, head north on Bd Lorrain/QC-366 O for 850 m and turn right onto Rue des Fleurs. After 600 m turn left onto Rue des Jacinthes where the bridge is 350 m
Crosses: Rivière Blanche
Carries: N/A
Builder: Not known
Year Built: 2016
Truss Type: Town variation
Dimensions: 1 Span, 28 meters, 92 feet
Notes: This bridge was built on the White River trail for pedestrians and cyclists. It is the third covered bridge on the trail with plans for one more. It was named for the volunteers

World Index Number: QC/61-25-36
Formerly Listed in County: Gatineau

Pont Félix-Gabriel-Marchand
Region: Outaouais, Québec
Township: Mansfield

GPS Position: 45°51'41.0"N 76°44'26.0"W
Directions: From Mansfield-et-Pontefract, head northwest on QC-148 O for 1.2 km and turn left onto Chem. du Pont Rouge and the bridge
Crosses: Rivière Coulonge
Carries: Chem. du Pont Rouge
Builder: Augustus Brown
Year Built: 1898 (R12964) (R1997) (R2021)
Truss Type: Town and Queen
Dimensions: 6 Spans, 152 meters, 499 feet
Notes: This is the longest covered bridge in the province. It was named for Félix-Gabriel Marchand, prime minister of Québec. It was restored in 1964, 1997 and 2021.

World Index Number: QC/61-53-01
Formerly Listed in County: Pontiac

Pont du Faubourg
Region: Saguenay-Lac-Saint-Jean, Québec
Township: Saint-Jean

GPS Position: 48°14'05.0"N 70°12'10.0"W
Directions: From Les Trois-Ponts, head north on Rue Saint-Jean-Baptiste for 2.7 km and turn left onto Rue du Faubourg where the bridge is 250 m
Crosses: Rivière Saint-Jean
Carries: Rue du Faubourg
Builder: Not known
Year Built: 1929 (R1986)
Truss Type: Town variation
Dimensions: 1+ Span, 37 meters, 122 feet
Notes: The 1986 repairs were needed when the bridge was carried away by an ice jam. After repairs, it was returned to its site by transport truck. The central pier is a later addition.

World Index Number: QC/61-17-01
Formerly Listed in County: Chicoutimi

Pont du Lac-Ha! Ha!
Region: Saguenay-Lac-Saint-Jean, Québec
Township: Boilleau

GPS Position: 48°04'00.0"N 70°49'27.0"W
Directions: From Boilleau, head south on QC-381 S for 2.2 km and turn right onto Chem. du Pont Couvert/Rte Ancienne 381 and find the bridge
Crosses: Rivière Ha! Ha!
Carries: Chem. du Pont Couvert/Rte Ancienne 381
Builder: Not known
Year Built: 1934
Truss Type: Town variation
Dimensions: 2 Spans, 37 meters, 122 feet
Notes: This bridge has been closed since the summer of 2010. It is the only covered bridge in Quebec whose panels are corrugated sheet metal. The bridge is currently green with white mouldings. It was formerly white with red mouldings
World Index Number: QC/61-17-04
Formerly Listed in County: Chicoutimi

Pont Rouge (Sainte-Jeanne d'Arc)
Region: Saguenay-Lac-Saint-Jean, Québec
Township: Dolbeau

GPS Position: 48°52'59.0"N 72°05'05.0"W
Directions: From Sainte-Jeanne-d'Arc, head NW on Chem.
Principal for 1.6 km and turn left onto Rte du Pont Couvert.
After 1.1 km turn left onto Chem. du Pont Couvert and see the
bridge
Crosses: Rivière Noire
Carries: Chem. du Pont Couvert
Builder: Not known
Year Built: 1936 (R1995) (R2013)
Truss Type: Town variation
Dimensions: 1 Span, 25 meters, 82 feet
Notes: Major repairs were needed in 1995 due to damage
from an arson attack. An extensive rehabilitation was done in
2013. It is closed in winter.
World Index Number: QC/61-60-04
Formerly Listed in County: Roberval

Abiti-Est County Tour

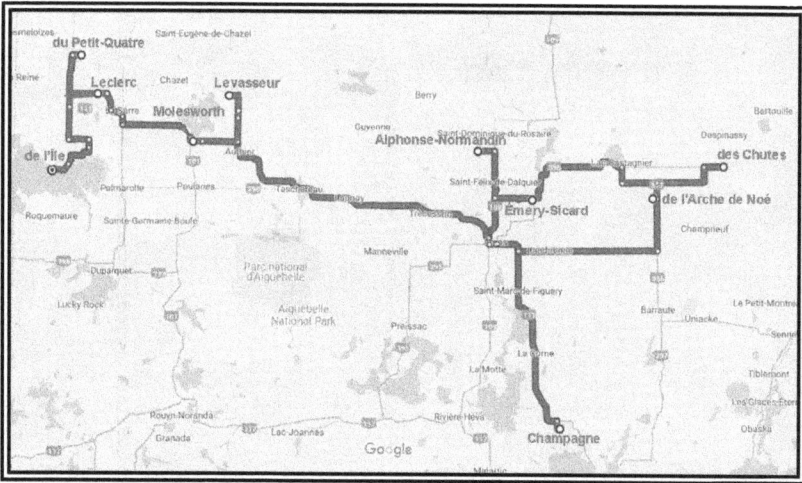

10 Bridges with 5 hours 20 minutes driving

Pont Champagne (Vassan)	48°12'53.0"N 77°55'32.0"W
Pont Alphonse-Normandin	48°44'04.0"N 78°09'49.0"W
Pont Émery-Sicard	48°38'36.0"N 78°00'18.0"W
Pont des Chutes	48°42'17.0"N 77°26'41.0"W
Pont de l'Arche de Noé	48°38'46.0"N 77°39'03.0"W
Pont Levasseur	48°50'07.0"N 78°53'22.0"W
Pont Molesworth	48°44'56.0"N 78°59'39.0"W
Pont Leclerc	48°50'11.0"N 79°16'33.0"W
Pont du Petit-Quatre	48°54'29.0"N 79°19'35.0"W
Pont de l'Île	48°41'30.0"N 79°24'27.0"W

Abiti-Ouest County Tour

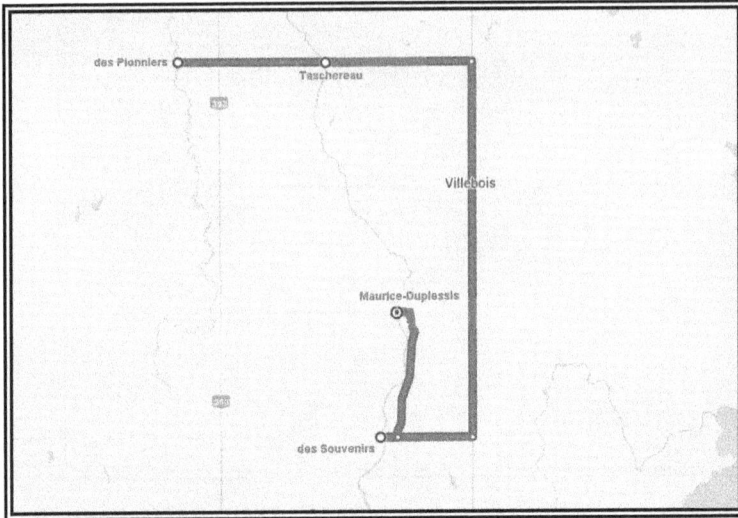

4 Bridges and 30 minutes driving

Pont des Pionniers	49°07'35.8"N 79°15'16.6"W
Pont Taschereau	49°07'35.0"N 79°12'03.0"W
Pont des Souvenirs	49°02'18.9"N 79°10'50.9"W
Pont Maurice-Duplessis	49°04'04.0"N 79°10'30.0"W

Compton County Tour

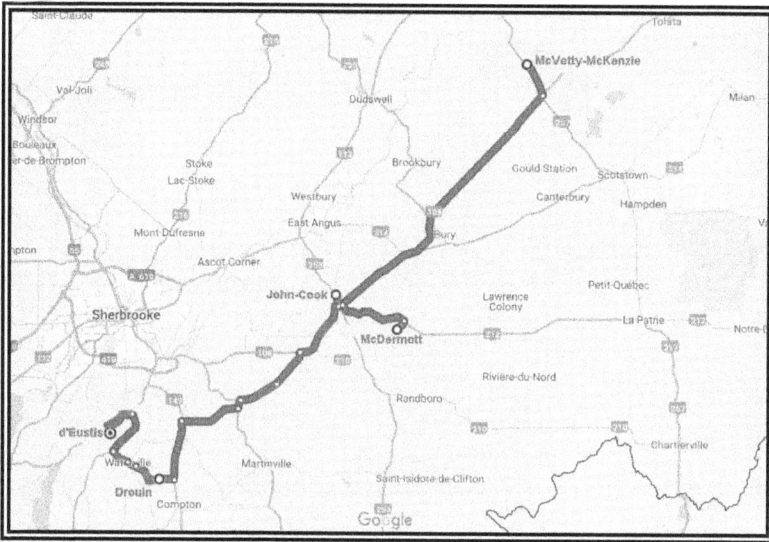

5 Bridges with 1 hour 15 minutes driving

McVetty-McKenzie	45°37'10.0"N 71°23'42.0"W
McDermott	45°23'34.0"N 71°33'22.0"W
John-Cook	45°25'19.0"N 71°37'57.0"W
Drouin	45°15'50.0"N 71°51'05.0"W
d'Eustis	45°18'11.0"N 71°54'48.0"W

Gatineau County Tour

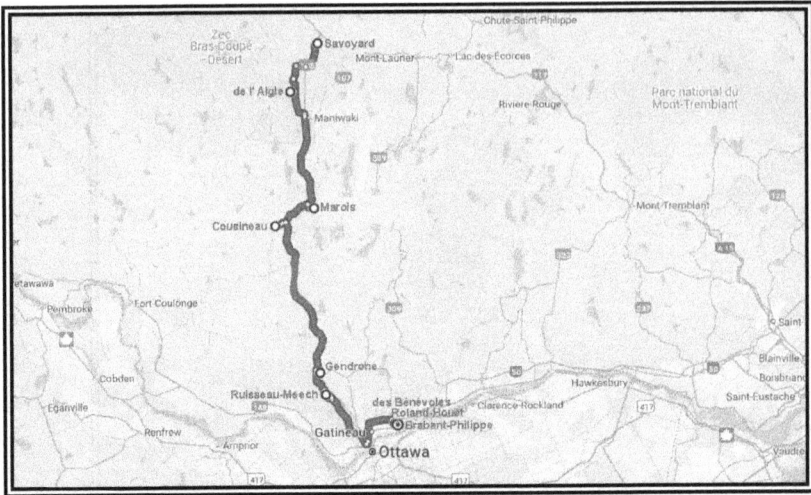

9 Bridges with 3 hours driving

Savoyard (Grand-Remous)	46°35'30.0"N 75°55'48.0"W
de l' Aigle	46°27'10.0"N 76°02'41.0"W
Marois	46°07'07.5"N 75°56'37.1"W
Cousineau	46°03'57.0"N 76°06'27.0"W
Gendrone (Wakefield)	45°38'44.6"N 75°55'06.2"W
Ruisseau-Meech	45°34'57.0"N 75°53'45.0"W
des Bénévoles	45°30'11.2"N 75°36'02.0"W
Roland-Houét	45°29'59.5"N 75°36'16.3"W
Brabant-Philippe	45°29'54.0"N 75°35'39.0"W

Labelle County Tour

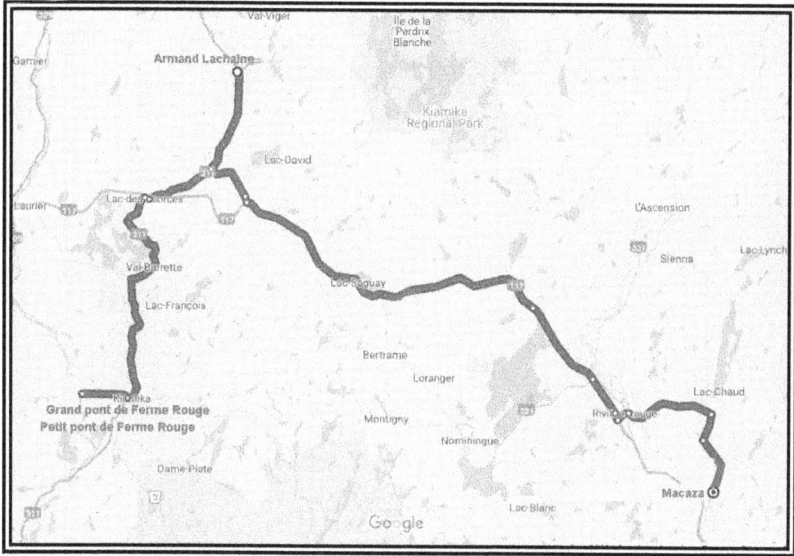

4 Bridges with 1 hour 30 minutes driving

Grand pont de Ferme Rouge   46°25'35.0"N 75°25'44.5"W
Petit pont de Ferme Rouge   46°25'35.1"N 75°25'40.0"W
Armand Lachaîne   46°38'36.0"N 75°16'08.0"W
Macaza   46°21'24.0"N 74°46'46.0"W

Matane County Tour

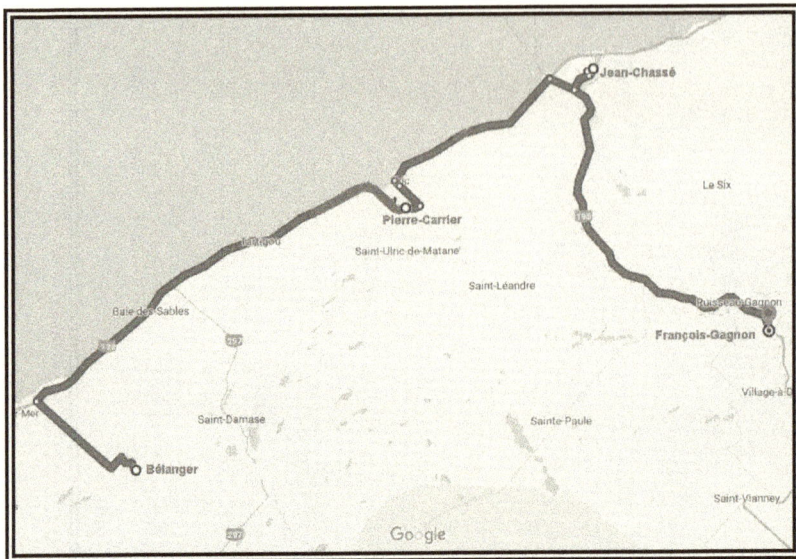

4 Bridges with 1 hour driving

Bélanger (Les Boules)	48°38'08.0"N 67°54'20.0"W
Pierre-Carrier	48°46'20.0"N 67°41'05.0"W
Jean-Chassé (St. Luc)	48°43'12.0"N 67°24'50.0"W
François-Gagnon	48°42'24.0"N 67°23'22.0"W

Matapédia County Tour

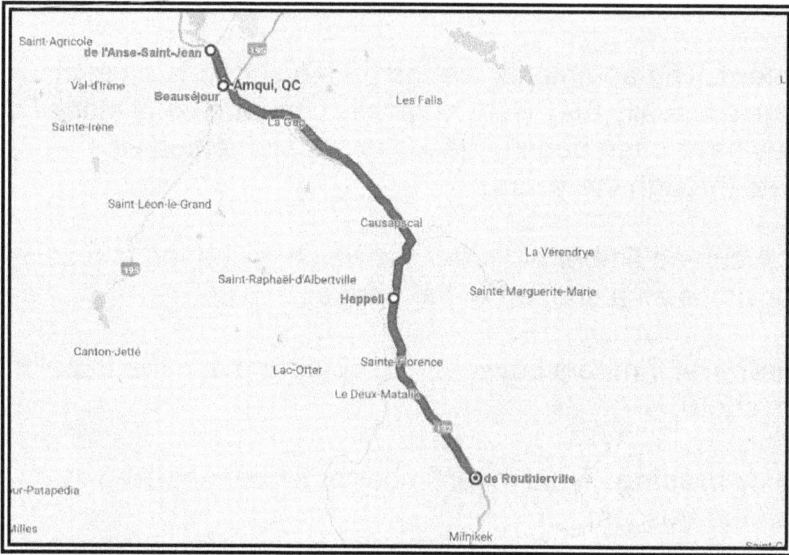

4 Bridges with 45 minutes driving

de l'Anse-Saint-Jean (Amqui)	48°29'31.0"N 67°26'54.0"W
Beauséjour	48°27'58.0"N 67°26'00.0"W
Heppell	48°18'43.0"N 67°14'29.0"W
de Routhierville	48°10'56.0"N 67°08'57.0"W

Glossary

Abutment: The abutments are the bridge supports on each side bank. Usually they were originally constructed of stone but they have often been replaced or supplemented with concrete through the years.

Arch: A curved timber or timber set which is shaped in a curve and functions as a support of the bridge.

Bed timbers: Timbers between the abutment and the truss or bottom chord.

Brace or bracing: A diagonal timber or timber set used to support the trusses.

Bridge Deck: The roadway through the bridge.

Buttress: Wood or metal members on the exterior sides which connect the floor beams and the top of the truss. Used to keep the bridge structure from twisting under wind, water and snow loads.

Camber: A planned curve in the structure to compensate for the weight of the structure.

Chord: The horizontal members extending the length of the truss meant to carry the load to the abutments.

Dead load: The load of the weight of the bridge itself.

Deck: The pathway through the bridge used by pedestrians or vehicles.

Pier: Stone/concrete supports built in the stream bed to support the bridge

Portal: The bridge's entrances.

Post: The truss's vertical members.

Span: The bridge length measured between the abutments.

Treenails or trunnels: Pins or dowels turned from hardwood, driven into holes drilled into the members of the truss to hold them together. Also used in mortised joints.

Truss: The framework which carries the load of the bridge and distributes it to the abutments.

Truss Types

A Truss is a system of ties and struts which are connected to act like a single beam to distribute and carry a load. In covered bridges, these Trusses carry the load to stone abutments at each side and perhaps piers in between.

Brown

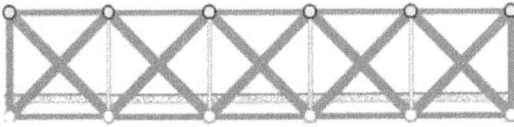

Brown

Josiah Brown Jr., of Buffalo, New York, patented this system in 1857.It consists of diagonal cross compression members connected to horizontal top and bottom stringers and is known for economic use of materials. It was only used in Michigan where there are a couple of surviving members.

Burr Arch

Burr Arch

Invented in 1804 by Theodore Burr, the Burr Arch is one of the most commonly found structures in Covered Bridge design. It is often used in combination with multiple kingposts. The ends of the arch are buried in the abutments

Childs

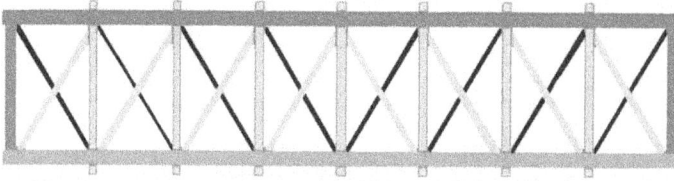

Childs

The Childs Truss System is essentially a multiple kingpost with half of the diagonal timbers replaced with iron bars.

Howe

Howe Truss

The Howe Truss was patented in 1840 by William Howe. It involves the use of vertical metal rods between the joints of wooden diagonals.

Kingpost

Kingpost Truss

Kingpost is the simplest form of Truss with two diagonal members on a bottom chord, often with a vertical post connecting to the diagonals. The multiple Kingpost involves a series of Kingposts symmetrical from the bridges center. This allows for a much longer span.

Long

Long

The Long Truss was patented by Stephen Long in 1830. It is a series of X shaped diagonals connected to vertical posts

Paddleford

Paddleford

Peter Paddleford worked with the Long Truss system and eventually adapted it with a system of interlocking braces. he was never able to patent the system due to challenges from the owners of the Long Truss patent. However there are a number of New Hampshire and Vermont bridges which use the Paddleford system

Partridge

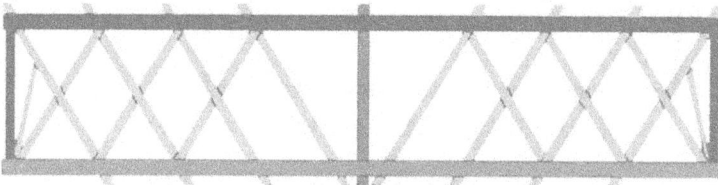

Partridge

Reuben L. Partridge received a patent for a design similar to the Smith system but adding terminal braces at the end and a central vertical member.

Pratt

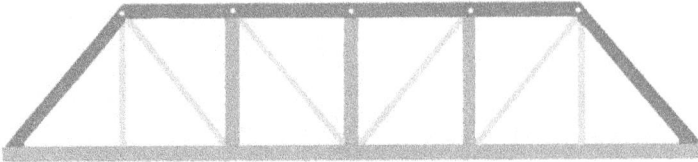

Pratt

The Pratt truss was patented in 1844 by Caleb Pratt and his son Thomas Willis Pratt. The design uses vertical members for compression and horizontal members to respond to tension.

Queenpost

Queenpost Truss

The Queenpost has the peak of the kingpost type replaced with a horizontal top chord which allows for a longer span.

Smith

Smith Truss

Robert W. Smith received patents in 1867 and 1869 for variations of his system.

Town

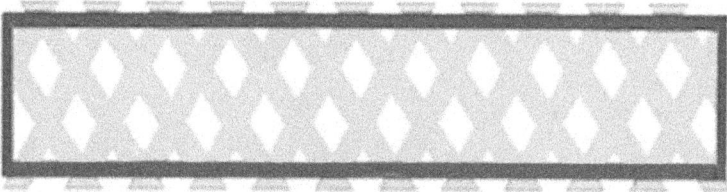

Town Truss

The Town or lattice system was patented by Ithiel Town in 1820. It involved a system of overlapping diagonals in a lattice pattern connected at the intersection by Tree nails or trunnels, wooden pegs or dowels. It had the advantages in that it could be constructed by unskilled labour and local materials could be used.

Warren

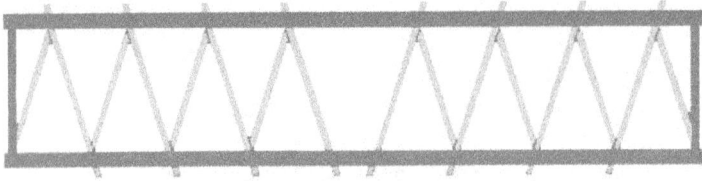

Warren

Patented in 1848 by two Englishmen, one of whom was named James Warren, it consists of parallel upper and lower chords with diagonal connecting members forming a series of equilateral triangles.

Recently Lost

British Columbia
Ashnola River Road, BC/52-21-02, Burned Sept 2014

New Brunswick
Adair, NB/55-02-01x, Lost to Arson October 14, 2009
Keenan, NB/55-02-08x, Burned 3 May 2001
Mangrum, NB/55-02-10x, Lost to Arson 13 Aug 2011
St. Nicholas River, NB/55-05-08x, Burned 25 Feb 2001
Aaron Clark, NB/55-09-02x, Flood April 16, 2014
Irish River #1, NB/55-11-05x, Demolished 27 Sep 2021
Bell, NB/55-12-01x, Flood 17 Jan 2018
Tay Falls, NB/55-15-08x, Lost to Arson 11 Oct 2008

Quebec
Saint-Félix-de-Dalquier, QC/61-01-21x, Lost to arson, 2006
Carrier, QC/61-01-28x, Burned 18 Aug 2011
du Canton Laas, QC/61-01-30x, Collapsed 2011
Davy, QC/61-01-U01x, Arson 23 Sep 2020
de La Calamité, QC/61-02-04x, Lost to arson May 31, 2021
Blanc, QC/61-02-P01x, Burned 2019
de la Traverse, QC/61-02-P11x, Flood 2012
Kelly, QC/61-25-13x, Lost to Arson January 19, 2019
Coulée-Carrier, QC/61-42-03x, Flood 17 Nov 2007
Gareau, QC/61-46-01x, Collapsed Sep 2011
de Capelton, QC/61-67-02x, Lost to Arson, 19 Sept 2002

References

National Society for the Preservation of Covered Bridges
http://www.coveredbridgesociety.org

New York State Covered Bridge Society
http://www.nycoveredbridges.org

Vermont Covered Bridge Society
http://www.vermontbridges.com/

Covered Bridge Society of Oregon
http://www.covered-bridges.org/

The Theodore Burr Covered Bridge Society of Pennsylvania
http://www.tbcbspa.com/

Indiana Covered Bridge Society
http://www.indianacrossings.org/

Ohio Historic Bridge Association
http://oldohiobridges.com/ohba/index.htm

Harold Stiver Image Gallery
https://haroldstiver.smugmug.com/Galleries/Themes/Covered-Bridges

Photo Credits:

British Columbia Bridges
Ymblanter, Kicking Horse Pedestrian
All other Images are by the author

New Brunswick Bridges
C Hanchey, Moores Mill ; **Cornellier**, Wheaton: **Dennis Jarvis**, Hartland, Sawmill, Vaughan Creek; **Gillian**, Starkey , **Gisling**, Hartland, **James Mann**, Canaan, **James Walsh**, Bamfort Colpitts, Peter Jonah; **New Brunswick Public Domain**, Florenceville; **R.L'Heureux**, Quisibis River
All other Images by the author

Ontario Index
All Images are by the author

Quebec Covered Bridges
Amqui, Jean-Chassé, François-Gagnon; **Csapbat**, La Macaza; **Fralambert**, Bordeleau, de Saint-Mathieu, de Saint-Edgar, Heppell, Romain-Caron, Taschereau; **Guerinf**, Armand, Champagne; **JeffT**, Rouge; **Johny-le-cowboy**, ste-jeanne-darc; **Khayman**, Belanger; **Pascal721,** Denommee, Bolduc, Landry, Levasseur, de l'Arche-de-Noé; **Michel Rathwell**, Beauséjour; **R. L'Heureux**, Saint-Andre; **RaynaultM**, de Wakefield; **Yanick Pelletierm**, des Défricheurs, du Sault; **Ymblanter**, Pierre-Carrier
All other Images are by the author

The Photographer's and Explorer's Series

Unless noted, there are Print and eBook editions available for the following.

Birding Guide to Orkney
Guide to Photographing Birds

Maine Lighthouses
Ontario Lighthouses

Ontario's Old Mills

Ontario Waterfalls

Alabama Covered Bridges (eBook)
Canada's Covered Bridges
California Covered Bridges (eBook)
Connecticut Covered Bridges (eBook)
Georgia Covered Bridges (eBook)
Indiana Covered Bridges
Maine Covered Bridges (eBook)
Massachusetts Covered Bridges (eBook)
Michigan Covered Bridges (eBook)
New Brunswick Covered Bridges
New England Covered Bridges
Covered Bridges of the Mid-Atlantic
Quebec Covered Bridges
Covered Bridges of the South
Missouri Covered Bridges
New Hampshire Covered Bridges
New York Covered Bridges
Ohio's Covered Bridges
Oregon Covered Bridges

The Covered Bridges of Kentucky (eBook)
The Covered Bridges of Kentucky and Tennessee
The Covered Bridges of Tennessee (eBook)
Vermont's Covered Bridges
The Covered Bridges of Virginia (eBook)
The Covered Bridges of Virginia and West Virginia
Washington Covered Bridges (eBook)
The Covered Bridges of West Virginia (eBook)
West Coast Covered Bridges

Indexes

www.ingramcontent.com/pod-product-compliance
Lightning Source LLC
Chambersburg PA
CBHW030927090426
42737CB00007B/348

9 781927 835425